Lewis Carroll told us about Wonderland. In this collection of ironic tales, Rubacher tells us of another Wonderland. The magic of Thailand is captured again and again.
Ian Quartermaine, *Sleepless In Bangkok.*

The author refuses to identify the Thai Samantha in the story "Sex And The City Goes Thai." He is respecting her wish to remain anonymous. I am an investigative journalist and will track her down.
Rajiv Bhattachargee, Bangkok.

Thai Touch displays a lovely Thai woman on the cover. That's the first touch. The second is the author dedicating his book to the Thai people and culture . . . a very Buddhist way of showing gratitude. The third touch is the book itself—very amusing and entertaining. It touches the heart.
Prof. Sman Ngamsit,
Dean of Graduate School, Siam University.

Thai Touch

Thai Touch

Richard Rubacher

PAIBOON

PUBLISHING

Published by

Paiboon Poomsan Publishing
582 Amarinniwate Village 2
Nawamin 90 (Sukha 1) Bungkum
Bangkok 10230
Thailand.
Tel: 662-509-8632; Fax: 662-519-5437

Paiboon Publishing
PMB 256, 1442A Walnut Street
Berkeley, California 94709
USA.
Tel: 1-510-848-7086; Fax: 1-510-666-8862

Info@paiboonpublishing.com
www.paiboonpublishing.com

Cover Design: Doug Morton

The names of some real characters
have been changed where requested.

Printed in Thaland.

ISBN 1-887521-69-0

*Dedicated to
the Thai people, Thai culture,
the fruits and vegetables of the land,
the fish in the sea, the elephants, and
the hundreds of monkeys who have
taken over the town of Lopburi.*

Contents

Acknowledgements

To ALL of my Thai teachers. Despite their best efforts, I continue to be a language basket case, although they say otherwise—Chocolate, Aree, Nui, Nut, Wiyada, Angel Face, and Nusara.

My editor, Mr. Baker.

Joker John Hudson, who provided me with insights galore and introduced me to his far-out friends who visit the kingdom.

Joker John's wife, Suvatthana (Suzy), who has given me an insider's understanding of Thai culture.

Jim Platzek, who kept urging me to visit the magical kingdom. I came, I saw, and I stayed.

The two Expats Clubs in Pattaya. Both groups honor the spirit of their slogan—"Expats helping expats."

All my koffee klatch dudes at The Lagoon restaurant at Omni Tower on Sukhumvit Soi 4—Dale Metcalf; Tony Pineda; Antoine the Frenchman; Roger, the Swiss currency trader; Steve Weisberg, the photographer; Sande Cohen, the far-out professor; Michael Sorenson, who directs his films with loving kindness; Daniel, the charming American actor who lives in Bangkok; Michelle, the Aussie (and, so far, the only dudess among the dudes); and the other visiting novelists, filmmakers, and friends who stay at the Omni during their visits, and the waitresses who take care of us.

Welcome To The Magical Kingdom Of Thailand

I REMEMBER the Ray Charles interview on the BBC TV program "Hard Talk," hosted by Tim Sebastian. The legendary singer was asked which of the 168 countries he had visited was free from racism. Without a moment's hesitation, he said, "Every country has its dark side."

Tim Sebastian asked him to elaborate.

"Every country has its shame and dirty linen. The dark side can be anything from racial, religious, economic, or class discrimination. Every country has its own version of corruption. No country on the planet is without fault."

But it might be said that some countries have more light than others, and that some are dimly lit.

1

Beauty In The Magical Kingdom

In Thailand, beauty surrounds you. Beauty embraces you. Beauty breathes its spirit into your heart. One example of beauty is found in the Thai *wat* ('temple'). Sometimes I am unable to tell if I am seeing a fabled kingdom in a dream state, such is the intoxicating experience when gazing at one of the temples in the Land of Smiles.

One writer, Steven M. Newman, reported in *Travelers' Tales: Thailand*: "As beautiful as they were in the sunlight, the graceful and intricately adorned spires and columns of the more elaborate *wats* took on a fairy-tale quality in the late hours of the night. Their brightly colored porcelain, ceramic, and gold reflected the lights of both the city and the moon as if they had been dusted by a magical wand."

One of my favorite authors, Somerset Maugham, lit the torch that inflamed my imagination. Spellbound by what he saw of Bangkok, he gave us an awe-inspiring description of the land- and waterscape. At twilight, from his view on the veranda of the Oriental Hotel, he looked at the Chao Phraya River and painted this picture: "A flight of egrets flew down the river, flying low and scattered. They were like a ripple of white notes, sweet and pure and spring-like, which an unseen hand drew forth, like a divine arpeggio from an unseen harp."

Maugham, in prose, makes a musical splash in our awareness. I am convinced that he was familiar with Plato's observation that "music gives charm to sadness and a life to everything."

It is an honor and a privilege to hang out in the kingdom that is a tonic for the soul. What follows are more reasons why I continue to be enchanted with the bright side of the Land of Smiles and disenchanted with the dark. My sourness, however, is always short-lived, as the charm of the Thai culture and people propel me back to enchantment.

To paraphrase Elizabeth Barrett Browning: Thailand, why do I love you? Let me count the ways.

Thai Good Luck Charms

Topping the list of good luck charms in the kingdom is, of course, Lord Buddha.

Buddha, Buddha, Buddha. Everywhere Lord Buddha—in temples, taxis, shop windows, bookstores, airports, on street vendors' carts, on shrines in front of homes, apartment complexes, and many office buildings. Lord Buddha is also displayed on necklaces, anklets, bracelets, earrings, tie clips, belt buckles, and T-shirts.

One other object that is revered is none other than the male reproductive organ, which is regarded as sacred. Thais, male and female alike, have a special attraction to the boisterous fella. It is seen as a symbol of power, fertility, and prosperity. One woman, a columnist on Thai culture, told me that she adores the phallus, whether it is a carving or the real thing. "The bigger and fatter the phallus, the more I am enthralled," she said. After making suggestive sounds, she added, "I like to touch power."

Thai Playfulness

There is a saying, *khon Thai kii len*. 'Thai people are playful.' The language itself is playful. The word for 'socks' is *tuung tao* ('bag for

feet'). 'Sweater' is a combination of *suea* ('shirt') and *naao* ('cold').
Thus we have a garment for cold weather.

An example of playful people in a playful culture is found in
chue len—'nicknames.' The literal meaning of *chue len* is 'name play.'
The quixotic names, especially for girls, show the sense of humor
that pervades Thai culture. A good friend of mine, a waitress at the
condominium where I lived for one year, is named Pak (Vegetable).
There is also Ngoo (Snake), Plaa (Fish), Goong (Shrimp), Nok (Bird),
Goy (Pinky), Gai (Chicken), Neung (Number One) and Lek (Little).
There is Yai (Big) and Yui (Chubby). Some boys may be blessed with
the name of Prik (Chilli). But, on the other hand, a girl may be lucky
enough to be called Naam Waan (Syrup).

One couple I know named their baby girl, Aay (Shy, pronounced
'eye'). Mother explained, "Baby did not want to come out. Too shy."
When Shy was one month shy of her second birthday, her mother
said, "She not *aay* anymore."

A university student I met on a train trip told me her nickname
was Beer. I asked how that came about. "My mom and dad are good
drinking buddies," she said. "During pregnancy, mother had to give
up beer. When I was born, she and my dad celebrated with—"

A waitress in one of my favorite restaurants is named Moi. She
was too polite to tell me that I was using the wrong speech tone
when I called her over to take my order. On many occasions, Thai
people in the restaurant would giggle when they heard me call her.
One day, a Thai man asked if he could talk to me about an urgent
matter. I invited him to join me. He told me there is *moi* in a high
tone and *moi* in a rising tone. The waitress's name is said with a high

tone. I was saying her name in a rising tone, which means 'pubic hair.' I thanked him for the correction.

One way to have fun without causing harm or distress is when ordering a drink at a posh restaurant or nightclub. "May I have a glass of 'Five Phallus Wine' please?"

"A glass of what?" the waitress asks.

"'Five Phallus Wine' please."

"You joking, yes?"

"Not joking. It's called 'Five Phallus Wine.'"

"Excuse one moment, please."

At this point she scurries away and chats with one or two other waitresses or with the manager. She returns with her colleagues or the manager. I am asked to write down on a pad what I would like to drink. I oblige.

By this time, the word is out. Other staff hover near my table, politely eavesdropping, pretending to be occupied. The waitress and manager try their best to be serious when the inevitable question is asked: "How to make this drink?"

"Very easy. Over a good wine in a cocktail shaker, you add the male organs of a cow, deer, dog, goat, and snake."

That's when the 'aha' moment comes. They know that I want to have the traditional Asian drink of all drinks—a supposed sexual enhancer. A cocktail Viagra.

"You want power, yes?"

This is when I know they are tuned in to *kii len* (the Thai zest for play). I am asked if the 'Five Phallus Wine' works for females.

"The power cocktail works for both sexes."

They chatter in Thai. Often a frenzy of excitement is reached. Others in the room are made privy to the conversation. Day or night, high places or low, frolicking and a sense of play dominate the cityscape.

Not Afraid Of Germs

During my first trip to the magical kingdom in 2000, I went to Chiang Rai, a provincial town in the north, near the Burmese border. Walking down the main street, I saw an attractive young woman sucking an ice-cream cone. Approaching the girl was a young mother holding the hand of her five- or six-year-old daughter. The woman with the ice-cream stopped and handed the cone to the little girl. Before accepting the gift, the girl smiled, gave a *wai*, and licked the delicious treat. The mother exchanged *wais* with the generous stranger and they all went on their way.

In the United States, this act of random kindness and senseless beauty would never take place. The American mother (or father) would be horrified. The first thought of the parent would be that the licked ice-cream was full of germs. Followed by the suspicion that this was a demonic trick being perpetrated—the cone was surely laced with a harmful substance; the 'generous' woman was only pretending to taste the ice-cream and was actually a dangerous lunatic.

Such trusting people in Thailand. There's elegance in the simplicity.

Hail The King

The Thai monarch is respected worldwide. Thai people, the Thai press, and foreigners agree that the country is in good hands with

King Rama IX. When His Majesty talks, people listen with respectful awe. On two occasions in the 1970s, and again in 1992, the Thai army massacred university students and democracy protestors, and imposed martial law. His Majesty made telephone calls and conducted meetings with military generals and police commanders. His Majesty suggested the military and police brass put pressure on the offending dictators to voluntarily step down for the good of the country. The behind-the-scenes machinations worked on each occasion. The dictators, upon discovering they had incurred the disfavor of His Majesty, resigned immediately, resulting in democratic elections. The despots gave up without firing another shot. Amazing Thailand.

The King of Thailand's full name—Phrabaatsomjetbawpaminth aramahabhumiboladulyadejmahittalathibetramatrpbawdeejackrinaru bawdinsiammintharthirajborummanatblopphit.

Not kidding. There are 48 syllables and 125 letters in His Majesty's name. The short version is King Bhumibol, or King Rama IX. Among other things, Rama IX's full name means that he is the protector of his people, the citizens of Siam.

His Majesty is a 'Renaissance Man.' He plays the saxophone and has improvised with jazz royalty. He also paints, *a la* Winston Churchill, and composes songs that touch the Thai heart. Does Rama IX speak English? He was born in 1927 in Cambridge, Massachusetts.

Thai Talk

Here's an example of Thai Talk: at Café Inn, Siam Square, I overheard a Thai woman talking to a Western gent. "How is your mother?" he asked.

"Five days ago, she catch jet plane to heaven."

"Do you mean she died?"

"Yes. She take jet plane to heaven."

"I'm sorry."

"Not be sorry. She have good ☐ ight."

Thai Talk can even enrich the English language. Another example: I took my mobile phone for servicing. Instead of telling me the phone was broken beyond repair, the clerk said, "Sorry, your phone tired."

A Thai financial consultant, married to an Englishman, has a ten-year-old son. Instead of saying she doesn't like to cook, she states her case in a convincing and colorful manner—"I die on stove."

The Thai Smile

There is the celebrated Thai smile. The first thing that comes to mind is the healing effect it produces. Walk down the street, whether it is in Bangkok or a small village, and don't be surprised if any person approaching you will pass with a smile. That person, whether male or female, young or old, displays his or her inner glow easily.

No one can have a 'bad hair day' in this magical kingdom. Perhaps the blues can jostle us for twenty, maybe for 23 hours. But not for the entire day. No matter who I pass on the street or see on the 'skytrain' or subway, I'm never surprised when I encounter a smile delicious. The worker at the Dunkin' Donuts counter, male or female, when serving coffee and donuts, displays a lovely smile that dissolves the blues. A clerk in the supermarket will escort you to the exact location where the item you seek is shown to you. He or she will smile on the journey to the proper aisle. This phenomenon made me ask Tony U-Thasoonthorn (See "Thailand's Spiritual Banker") "Why do Thai people smile?"

The 'spiritual banker' said, "We're a happy people, Richard. There's a simple Thai saying—'We have fish in the water, fruit on the trees, and rice in the fields. The people are happy."

The saying is carved on a stone pillar from the ancient city of Ayuthaya, the former capital of Siam.

A most unusual and curious event occurred when I began studying the written language. There are 32 vowels. Not a typo: *32* vowels in the Thai alphabet. Eight of the vowels require the speaker to smile when the sound is uttered. Stated another way, 25 percent of the time a Thai person speaks, he or she has to smile. If it's a long vowel, a big smile; if a short vowel, a little smile. If a vowel is followed by another vowel, a common occurrence, we get the full Thai treat—a delightful ear-to-ear smile. The smiling is the result of an unconscious process learned from infancy. A Thai baby sees its mother, father, and older siblings smiling when it is being spoken to, adoringly looked at, and tickled. The same occurs when friends and relatives play with and talk in nonsense syllables to the new arrival in the magical kingdom. This emotional outpouring of affection makes Thai baby happy. Baby talk and nonsense syllables are common to cultures worldwide, of course. The difference here is that Thai baby continues to be lavished with affection and given Thai tickles. As a result, Thai baby keeps its merry disposition.

Guess how many consonants there are in the Thai language? *Forty-four*. Not kidding. Two have been discarded—thank Lord Buddha!—

making it a mere 42 consonants that have to be memorized. The total number of letters in the alphabet is 74. In addition to the avalanche of vowels and consonants to master, there is the matter of dealing with the five speech tones that must be incorporated in the memory bank. It must be pointed out that even mean-spirited Thais have to use the same vowels. The mean-spirited ones also use polite phrases when ordering food. Example: *Kor khanom pang song phan laew kafe rohn sai nom noi khap* ('May I have two slices of toast and coffee with milk, thank you'). The *noi* is thrown into the request as an extra measure of politeness. This simple request contains three polite words.

Fun With Languages

When I talk to Thais, they get headaches. Or dizzy. Thais have trouble with the letter 'v.' Instead of 'vowel,' they say 'wowel.' To another Thai, the 'wowel' is uttered as 'wawa.' I never tire of hearing either version. Ask a Thai to say 'guava.' It comes out 'gwaa-wah.'

In one of the 18,590 Starbucks cafés in Bangkok, I struck up a conversation with a woman seated at the next table. In Thai, I asked what kind of work she did.

"I clock," she said in English.

Pointing to her watch, I asked if she worked in a clock shop.

"I no work clock shop."

Perhaps a jewelry shop?

"I no work jewelry shop."

I joined her at her table, took out my notepad, and asked her to spell out what kind of work she did. She obliged, spelling out her job: "C-L-E-R-K."

I asked if she worked for the government.

"Yes, in government office, I clock."

Her name was Lakyim, and now it was the government clock's turn to throw some Thai tongue twisters at me—which she did with glee. She asked me to say 'snake' in Thai (*ngoo*). No matter how many times I tried, the troublesome 'ng' sound was mispronounced. Lakyim became excited and had me try to utter *nang ngan* ('so-so') and *nan ngai* ('there it is'). Imagine that—two 'ng' sounds in each word. Back-to-back 'ng's'.

Lakyim, I found out, means Dimples. She inquired if I knew the names of the months. I nodded. She pleaded for me to say 'May' and 'November.'

"Easy," I said. "May is *Phrusajikaayon* and November is *Phrusaphaakhom.*"

"Very good," she said. "Except you say May for November and November for May."

Showing no mercy, she asked me to utter 'dog' (*maa*). It was a trick and a trap. My tonal utterance came out as 'horse.' The word *maa* has five tones that produce the words 'dog,' 'horse,' and 'come.' The other two tones have no meaning; they are there—you guessed it—for play purposes.

I was told there are two ways that Thais kiss. One is the Western way, mouth-to-mouth. The second, or Thai version, the *hom*, is done by pressing the mouth and nose against the other person's cheek and affectionately sniffing quickly. *Hom* also means 'smells good.'

I asked Chocolate, my 24-year-old Thai-language mentor, where the kiss was usually placed by her suitor. "On my cheek," she said.

"And how long does the sniff kiss last?" I asked.

"Two seconds."

I asked her how long a Western kiss might last.

"Mouth-to-mouth very long."

Curious, I egged her on. "Until cannot breathe," she said.

I conducted research to find out if my mentor was pulling my leg. I took a survey of university students, clerks, waitresses, Internet shop workers, and travel agents. To my surprise, ninety percent in the survey went on record as saying that two seconds is enough time for the sniff kiss. A total of four seconds when applied to both cheeks.

The purpose of the sniff kiss is to determine if the scent of the person is fragrant, agreeable, or unpleasant.

'Dentist' in Thai is *mor fan*, where *mor* means 'doctor' and *fan* means 'tooth.' Literally, 'tooth doctor.' My pronunciation is 'more fun.'

This is a sign I saw in a guesthouse bathroom: "Please don't put sanitary towel in toilet bowl. It caused trouble."

The Thai Heart

The heart of Thai culture is found in sayings about the heart. According to Christopher G. Moore, the author of *Heart Talk: Say What You Feel In Thai*, there are a thousand expressions that refer to the heart. One of them is *jai yen*. It is "the Thai equivalent of a stiff upper lip in the face of adversity or provocation. A person may have suffered an emotional setback or disruption, but he or she is able to feel (or give the appearance of feeling) collected and cool emotionally in the face of the problem. For example, Lek is stuck in a traffic jam for hours or has a □ at tire on the expressway. The key is the ability to remain in control. Lek does not panic when the tire blows out. Being stuck at the Asoke and Sukhumvit intersection for forty minutes does not cause her to explode."

A person with a good heart is known as possessing *jai dii*; a bad heart is *jai dam*.

Christopher G. Moore pleads his case on the importance of the 'heart' in Thai culture:

> *Heart or 'jai' is a powerful, pervasive and complex metaphor. In Thai you can experience and understand heart as black, cool, diamond, dry, fast, hot, lost, open, mixed-up, poor, turbulent, wasted or worried.*
>
> *Whether you are a doctor, dock worker, lawyer, factory worker, merchant or jack-of-all-trades, then you are pulling an oar in the same conceptual boat constructed from the same as everyone else in your language and culture. If you wish to row in the Thai conceptual boat, an understanding of 'jai' is indispensable.*

The Thai Sense Of Humor

This is everywhere, every day. An example comes when describing the *tuk-tuk*—the frail, three-wheeled motor vehicle with a canopy roof but no windows or doors—used as a taxi in Bangkok and several other cities in the kingdom. I was once told by one of the drivers: "*Tuk-tuk* turn right. *Tuk-tuk* turn left. *Tuk-tuk* turn over." Then the driver asked, with a Cheshire-cat grin, "You take *tuk-tuk*, yes?" How could I resist? We made many right turns and many left turns. But luckily no turn-overs.

THAI TOUCH

No Road Rage

What continues to amaze me is the absence of road rage among Thai drivers, whether they are taxi drivers, people in private cars, *tuk-tuk* drivers, bus drivers, van drivers, or *songthaew* drivers (a passenger pick-up truck with two rows of benches screwed to the floor). In the USA, when stuck in a *rot tit* ('traffic jam'), some Americans become furious. When a car cuts in front, fury is coupled with sound. Some, in their sound and fury, take demonic action. The common practice is to display anger. Remember the film *Changing Lanes*, starring Samuel L. Jackson and Ben Affleck? It's a thriller that starts out with an automobile mishap. Common courtesy and decency have become a lost art in American society, commented film critic Jeff Vice (no kidding—that's his real name) in response to the film.

Being furious or showing anger is common practice in the United States, the 'Land of Frowns.' But *jai yen* (possessing a 'cool heart,' or remaining 'calm' and serene in a difficult situation) is an honored trait in this earthly paradise of Thailand.

Lawyers Not Needed

What a striking difference between the US of A and Thailand when a traffic accident occurs. In the Land of Smiles, the matter can be settled immediately. The Thai police determine how much damage is done to the vehicle, or how much the hospital bill will come to (if there is an injury).

This on-the-spot medical and vehicular assessment is promptly taken care of. The victim is paid in cash. No lawyer necessary. No court appearance necessary. No anxiety about going to trial; no days off required from the job. Lawyer jokes are not understood in the kingdom.

Settling disputes without involving lawyers is a nice practice here, and should be considered as a new feature in the good 'ol USA.

Thai Politeness And Courtesy

The refined manners of the Thai people are known worldwide. Speaking in a soft tone is an attractive quality in Thai men, women, and children. By constant exposure to Thai culture, Westerners learn to talk softly, unconsciously mimicking and absorbing the culture of their hosts.

Signs And Slogans

Written on a restaurant menu was the entrée, "Rain blow trout." You could also try the "Chief's salad." A sign on a dry cleaning shop: "Drop your pants for best results." A sign on the beach when I, along with forty members of the salsa dance club I belong to, visited the fun island of Koh Samet: "Not to leave any thing on beach except footprint."

A young woman on the 'skytrain' had the following words emblazoned on her shirt: "For Rent."

I doubt if she knew the meaning.

Nose Jobs

Many Thais not only complain about the shape of their nose, they do something about it—by having it transformed through cosmetic surgery into a nose that looks Western.

I plead with my Thai friends who want to undergo the change. I say, "Be proud of your nose the way it is."

I tell them their ski-slope nose is the same as Bob Hope's. The pleading is in vain. Off they go to the hospital or clinic. The cost for becoming more *farang*-like is a mere 5,000 baht. But don't go to the exclusive Bumrungrad Hospital in the heart of the Sukhumvit. There, the price is five times more.

Snow White

One of the top-selling cosmetic items is skin whitener, in the form of creams, jellies, lotions, and salves. For those who can afford the Michael Jackson approach, the choice is injections under medical supervision.

In Bangkok and the central and northwestern provinces, the people are quite light-skinned. They consider themselves blessed. In Isaan (the poor northeastern provinces of Thailand) and in the southern provinces, where the sun is merciless, the people have darker complexions. Many consider themselves cursed.

"Dark not good," said Pumpkin, my first Thai girlfriend. She hailed from Nakhon Si Thammarat, 400 miles south of Bangkok. Pumpkin's salary as a garment designer was 10,000 baht a month. At the age of 28, that's considered a good salary. She spent 25 percent of her wages on cosmetic creams and skin whiteners—many of which contain dangerous chemicals that cause long-term damage.

Pumpkin was not convinced by my observation that her skin resembled a South Sea Islander. "Your skin," I said, "is *sii naam pheung*." ('Honey colored.')

Her comment was, "*Phit, sii dum.*" ('Wrong, the color is black.')

I began paying attention to the skin tones of Thai actors, models, and TV presenters. The overwhelming majority are light-skinned.

The word 'pumpkin' in Thai is *fuk thong*. At her request, I did not say her Thai name in public. In private, it was okay.

Dental Care And Cost

I never did like my upper bridge that was made by my dentist in California. When I smiled, it was obvious that I wore a partial upper plate. During my second visit to the Land of Smiles, I accidentally stumbled upon Mahidol University, where they have a dental school and clinic. That's where I found a professor of dentisty, Dr. Theerathavaj Srihavaj.

"Richard," he said, "call me by my nickname, Knock." He graduated from the NYU School of Dentistry.

On Christmas Day, 2003, I made my sixth visit to Dr. Knock. That's when he fitted me with my new partial. Finally, I could smile. It was a work of art. Dr. Knock personally supervised the lab workers while the plate was being made. He had me come back three times after the fitting to make sure that it was snug as a bug in a rug. The cost came to 300 US dollars. That included X-ray, impressions, construction, his valuable time, and post care. I use the word 'care' in its true meaning. The American dentist wouldn't dream of going to the lab to check out the progress of a partial or denture. The American price for the same, but inferior, work was 2,500 US dollars.

Dr. Knock, in his early forties, shares another characteristic of Thais: he looks 25. In the morning, he teaches dental students at the university. In the afternoon and early evening, he applies his skills to patients, Thai and foreign. He is in charge of the "Maxillofacial Prosthetics Program," meaning that he works with patients with facial disfigurements as a result of throat and mouth cancer. He works six days a week.

I asked him why he didn't take up private practice on New York City's Park Avenue, where many NYU grads have offices.

"I feel privileged to take care of unfortunate people in Thailand with facial disfigurements," he replied.

Mahidol University is subsidized by the government. Dr. Knock's Thai salary? Under 20,000 US dollars a year.

Dr. Theerathavaj Srihavaj is one of my all-time heroic figures. He's another reason why I love Thailand so much.

My good friend in Bangkok, Joker John Hudson, and his Thai wife, Suvattana (Suzy) decided to have dental implant work done. He chose Bangkok Christian Hospital, which has a dental department. Joker is extremely sensitive to being in a dental chair that has to be titled back. His extreme sensitivity to his head arched backwards results in uncontrollable gasping for breath. He underwent a bone graft, where tissue was taken from his hip (instead of the bone being removed from his jaw). The hip tissue was grafted in three places in his mouth.

Joker John's dentist, Dr. Somchai Sesstrisombat, trained in Thailand; he performed the hip surgery as well as the implant procedure.

Joker told me that he stayed in a private room at the Christian Hospital. An extra bed was provided so his wife could be with him before and after the surgery. "I still can't believe it," he told me when I visited him the evening after the operation. "The first night, the cost of the room was 55 US dollars. That includes Suzy's bed. The second night was 45."

He raved about the attention he received from Dr. Somchai before and after the surgery. He raved about the swarm of nurses that attended to him. "Phenomenal."

The Thai touch touched him.

The entire cost of the six implants, surgery, medications, installations of ten crowns, X-rays, and follow-ups would amount to less than 15,000 US dollars."

I asked how much it would cost in the States or Europe. The price would be three times as much, with "no loving warmth."

Like me, Joker John loves Thailand too much.

Health Care

A few years ago, "60 Minutes" broadcast a show about the skillful cosmetic surgical work performed in Bangkok's Bumrumgrad Hospital. The show quoted the prices, including hospital stay and aftercare benefits.

People from the USA, Europe, the Middle East, Latin America, China, Japan, and Korea pour into Bumrumgrad Hospital, and other city hospitals, every day. They are classified as 'medical tourists.' It's a booming business in Thailand. Women, especially, come to Thailand for cosmetic facial work, skin tucks, breast procedures, and other kinds of beauty enhancements and restoration. Sex-change operations are also done at Bumrumgrad.

Mission Hospital (AKA Seventh Day Adventist) is another medical institution in Bangkok that attracts people with diversified afflictions, as do the prestigious Chulalongkorn and Mahidol hospitals.

How are the Thai people taken care of? There is the 'Thirty Baht Plan' (75 cents). By joining the Plan, Thai citizens are entitled to ongoing treatment throughout the kingdom. The Plan is available at all the government hospitals and clinics.

Thailand is rich in fruit. As a vegetarian, I am delighted at the diversity of fruit that thrives in the tropical kingdom. Street vendors with pushcarts are common in all the cities. A plentiful serving of watermelon, pineapple, or cantaloupe is sliced up before your eyes by the street merchant. A bag of each costs only ten baht. The supermarkets proudly display fruits that I've never seen in the United States.

The Price Is Right

I live in Bangkok's Sukhumvit area, which is on the skytrain route and also near the new subway system. I rent a huge, one-bedroom apartment with three balconies for the unbelievable price of 15,000 baht a month. Sixty percent of the people living at the Saranjai Mansion ('Happy Place') are Thai. The rest are Western and Korean. The maintenance fee, and electric and water fees amount to 2,000 baht monthly. The high-rise condo building has an Olympic-sized pool, a fitness room, and a restaurant—from where food is delivered when I throw parties.

Skillful technicians and tradesmen are available at a moment's notice. When the kitchen faucet needed replacing, the office dispatched a plumber to my place on the tenth floor. After surveying the situation, he told me there was no hope for the faucet. It needed to be replaced. I asked how much the new faucet would cost.

"Three hundred baht."

"No kidding?"

"Not kid, you, sir."

I gave him the 300 baht (about seven US dollars). Within an hour, he rang my bell again. He had already picked up the replacement at nearby Robinson's department store, on Sukhumvit Road. It took him ten minutes to install the new device. I asked how much I owed for the installation, his time, and his trip to the store.

He told me I had already paid the full amount of 300 baht.

I gave him a 200 baht tip, for which he was grateful.

Amazing Thailand!

My friend, Jim Platzek, moved out of his small apartment in Bangkok, into a new home that he purchased for 46,000 US dollars. There are three storeys in the house. The living room, dining room, and kitchen are on the first floor. Also on the first level is a spacious patio with a secure wrought-iron gate. The second and third floors have two massive bedrooms that are separated by a long corridor. There are two full bathrooms and one half-bathroom. Elegant tiles adorn each of the three floors. Another attraction is the spiral stairway. Although Jim lives in an outlying district, he is a mere twenty-minute bike ride from the nearest subway station.

Tony, a friend from Italy, lives in a full-fledged mansion with gardens. A wall surrounds the mansion. Living in the servants' quarters are the handyman and his wife, who cooks and performs maid service, including washing and ironing. The maid gets into her husband's car and goes shopping for Tony. She knows what his favorite foods are—Italian and Thai. "No problem, Mister Tony, I cook Italian and Thai for you."

The handyman also doubles as a driver, which pleases Tony to no end.

The disadvantage for me is that Tony's mansion is in a remote section of Bangkok. The advantage for him is that "taxis are cheap here."

Guess how much Tony pays for his lavish living style?

Wrong. Guess again.

Wrong again.

His rent is 10,000 baht a month.

The husband-and-wife team earns 5,000 baht monthly. That includes living quarters.

Food prices are also low, whether dining out or shopping in supermarkets.

Tailor-Made Clothing

When Wanda Wonder, my friend from San Francisco, came to visit me in Bangkok, her first priority was: "Take me to those fab Indian tailors."

Since I live on Sukhumvit, I was able to show her a couple of dozen tailor shops within a two-minute radius of my place. All the specialists in clothing design are permanent citizens of Thailand of Indian descent. Wanda Wonder had suits made to measure, blouses, a leather jacket, and some other dresses. She raved about the expertise of the workers. She raved about the choice of fabrics, the colors and patterns, and the prices. "Richard," she said, "imagine how much all these would cost in the Bay Area."

During her visit, Wanda pointed out something that I had seen every day but had never registered on my mind. "The cars in Thailand," she said, "are polished clean, and they glow." How true. She also pointed out that dented fenders and cars that have been in accidents are never seen. Once again, how true. Even taxi drivers spit-polish their vehicles.

Returning to clothing—I have my own Indian tailor. Actually it's three brothers—Mack, David, and Ravi. They are located near the National Stadium in Bangkok. Next month, I will buy a made-to-measure white suit with a matching vest, *a la* John Travolta in *Saturday Night Fever*. The following month, I will talk about purchasing a James Bond suit.

Trusting Thais

At a health fair in Bangkok, I met a nurse by the name of Goong (Shrimp). She was giving free blood tests to the fair goers. I was taken by her beauty and charm. The next day, I called the hospital where she worked and asked to be connected to her office. It turned out she was about to go on holiday for a week and was not available.

"Is it okay to get Nurse Shrimp's mobile number?" I asked. I expected the answer to be 'no way, sir.'

"Are you a friend of Nurse Shrimp?"

I explained that I had met her at the health fair the day before, and that I would like to be her friend.

"Just a minute, sir."

In less than a minute, I was given her private mobile number. Thai people, so trusting.

When I phoned Nurse Shrimp, she asked how I got her mobile number. When I told her, she wasn't surprised that her number had been given out to a stranger. We dated for a month. Then she went to the UK for graduate training.

Older Men, Younger Women

About older men and Thai women: not only do older *farang* men chase younger Thai women, they also catch them. In Western countries, this practice, as we know, is referred to in a negative way—the 'dirty old man' syndrome.

My Thai tutor, Miss Chocolate (she calls me Vanilla), set me up on a date with one of her roommates, another 24-year-old beauty. In my favorite hair salon in Bangkok, my stylist set me up with one of her young staff. There is the inevitable 'battle of the sexes' in Thailand, but it differs from the battle in the Western world by taking on a quirky and quixotic flavor.

Thai Women's Garb

Thai women dress in a comely manner. Perhaps a 'seductive' manner is a better term. What a visual thrill it is to ride the skytrain, take the subway, and have a leisurely stroll around Siam Square or any other popular place. What a thrill to take coffee in a café and watch the passing beauty parade. Thai women dress to kill, leaving men in a constant state of arousal.

Thai Men

I must talk about Thai men. To me, they are a mix of Peter Sellers, Billy Crystal, Robin Williams, and Woody Allen. Whenever I get the opportunity to practice my Thai in my fractured tones, they howl. The howling occurs after they recover from the headache my speaking causes. The glee occurs when I give taxi and *tuk-tuk* drivers directions; or when I strike up a conversation with a random Thai gent on a bus ride; or when I talk with a street vendor who sells fruits or juices.

At the World Fellowship of Buddhists, while waiting in the corridor for my friend Jim Platzek to obtain information from a European staff member, a Thai gent asked me if he could be of assistance. I took the opportunity to get a free language lesson. I took out one of my Thai textbooks and went over some of the words and sentences that twisted my tongue. He tried his best not to laugh when I spoke. He had to look at the text to see what I was trying to say. When I thought I'd got the tones right, I closed the book and uttered three sentences that I had rehearsed. From his expression, I realized he had no idea what I was trying to say.

I opened the book and pointed to the three expressions. He said no matter how much I butchered spoken Thai, I should not abandon my studies.

I told him it was going on two years and I was still on first base.

"What does it mean, 'still on first base'?"

I told him it was slang for being at square one all over again.

He told me that what's important was *trying* to be understood rather than *being* understood.

"That's very kind, sir, but do you mean that I am a basket case?" I explained that phrase, too.

"Yes, you are a basket case." Then he added, "A colorful basket."

Another thing about Thai men is their amazing tolerance and lack of jealousy when they encounter attractive young Thai women in the company of *much older farangs*.

Party Every Day

In the Land of Smiles, every day is a celebration. This is evident among all classes of Thai people. For example, the vendors on bustling Sukhumvit Road spread a blanket on the sidewalk and proceed to have a picnic while waiting for the walk-by traffic to stop and purchase their wares—shirts, pants, pajamas, watches, pirated DVDs, porno movies, souvenirs, etcetera. At lunchtime, workers huddle together to enjoy each other's company while sharing various food items. 'Every day is a celebration' has meaning in the kingdom. *Sanuk* ('having fun') has a holy meaning. Thais do their best to inject *sanuk* into any situation, even work. In fact, the word *ngan* has two meanings: 'work' and 'party.'

One recent Sunday morning, I had to catch the bus to Pattaya, the seaside resort that is just a two-hour ride from Bangkok. I walked from my pad to the skytrain, to take me to the bus station. While waiting for the train to arrive, I heard laughter and singing on the street below. Curious, I peered over the railings and looked at the spectacle fifty feet below. Huddled together at the front of the Pasta & Noodles restaurant, at 6.15 in the morning, was a group of young women. They sat on the steps singing their favorite Thai tunes. I had no idea how they came to be assembled. Perhaps they were ladies of the night who had finished working and wanted to celebrate their good fortune of making money the night before.

Amazing Thailand!

As Ray Charles noted, every country has its dark side. Thailand is no exception. Implicit in the singer's observation is that every country also has its bright side. Thailand's plate is not only full when it comes to joy, celebration, merriment, and *sanuk*—the plate positively overflows.

As noted previously, my favorite four words that characterize the spirit of the Thai people are *khon Thai kii len* ('Thai people are playful'). One evening, after a business meeting with my publisher, we went to her favorite restaurant on Sukhumvit. It was my first time there. After she placed her order, the waitress turned to me. I decided to conduct a test. In my improved Thai, I said, "*Phom mai hew, khrap. Kor kafe rohn lek, sai nom mai sai naam plaa noi khrap.*" ('I'm not hungry, but could I please have a small coffee with milk, but no fish sauce.')

The waitress howled, as did my publisher.

The waitress repeated my order to her colleagues. Laughter resounded in the restaurant.

"Thai people are playful," I said to my publisher.

"And so are you," she said as Thai customers joined the chorus of delight.

A toast to Thailand!

Thai Breasts
And The Government

WHEN KHEMMIKKA NA SONGKHLA was seventeen, she became distraught—with the visual evidence that her breasts were so small as to be non-existent. In desperation, she began using breast-firming cream to massage her breasts into shape. Her grandmother, then 74, told her that the cream alone wouldn't be effective without the right type of massage.

Her grandmother unlocked a secret that changed Khemmikka's life in unexpected ways. The old woman taught her some "breast slapping" exercises and the ritual of splashing cold water onto the breasts at the end of the exercise. This 'Songkran of the breasts' toned the pectoral muscles and increased circulation in the desired area.

A confirmed skeptic, Khemmikka irregularly practiced the regimen over a two-year period. Her skepticism gave way to wonder. "One day, I saw the difference," she said.

At twenty, the enterprising Khemmikka opened a beauty salon and introduced the 'Songkran of the breasts' and the breast-slapping technique to her customers. To her delight, customers reported that their breasts became firmer and bigger. She made international headlines, attracting small-breasted women from Japan, Hong Kong, Singapore, Taiwan, the UK, and the USA. American and British women, worried about the perils of breast implants, flocked to Bangkok to undergo the six-day training program.

There was money in this venture: 360 US dollars per customer from foreign shores. A "Thai breast therapist" is how she was dubbed by the media.

Two years into her venture, one of Khemmikka's customers was diagnosed with breast cancer. There was suspicion that breast massage was the cause.

Khemmikka halted the program. She consulted Dr. Pennapha Sapcharoen, a director at the Institute for Traditional Thai Medicine, to determine if her method was the culprit. Dr. Pennapha stated that she could not give a medical opinion on the matter. The director of the Institute decided to research the effectiveness of 'breast slapping' and 'breast Songkran.'

Between August 2001 and January 2002, a study was conducted on forty women aged twenty to sixty. The results upheld Khemmikka's claims that breasts can be expanded and toned. No evidence that the method could cause breast cancer was detected.

As a result, a free program was launched for the public. For those who wanted better breasts, but were concerned about medical mishaps, the massage method guaranteed no cosmetic surgery, no damaging of breasts from invasive intrusions into a woman's body, no havoc with internal organs.

According to Kanchana Deewises, who helped develop the exercise regimen for the Department of Thai Traditional Medicine, the technique requires women to suck in their stomach during the exercises. This allows the abdominal muscles to act as a sort of "natural brassiere."

The Thai Ministry of Public Health is the umbrella agency that houses the Department of Thai Traditional Medicine in a sprawling governmental complex in Nonthaburi province on the outskirts of Bangkok. They point out ten benefits from the bust training program:

The bust enhancement or reduction program is safe for Thai women as it does not involve expensive and sometimes dangerous cosmetic surgery.

No hormone pills or toxic chemicals are used.

The regimen can act as an early cancer detection system. By massaging the breasts on a daily basis, women are able to see or feel if an abnormality is present.

The program promotes full body health. Volunteers undergoing the training acquire skills in acupressure points. By following the meridians (energy lines along the body) through using the thumb, wrist, and elbow, toning and strengthening of the arms, legs, neck, and head are enhanced.

Women who religiously follow the program will be in better health by developing a stronger immune system than women who do not exercise.

Part of the training involves aerobic exercises (including jumping rope and climbing steps). This aspect promotes cardio-vascular strengthening of the body.

The second phase of the training promotes traditional Thai yoga postures called *rusi dai ton*. This promotes mental well-being, spiritual serenity, and self-esteem.

Small breasts become bigger and firmer. Big breasts are reduced and sagging disappears. Cleavage is promoted, as the exercises are designed to bring the breasts closer together, bringing cleavage out of hiding.

The Thai economy is stimulated when foreign bras are forsaken for Thai-made bras. According to Dr. Pennapha, foreign bras are designed for Western women, whose body shape differs from Thai woman. Dr. Pennapha believes that foreign bras can deform Thai breasts. The economy is further stimulated when local people are involved in the design and manufacture of Thai-made bras.

When positive results are achieved, volunteers will teach 'Better Busts' to family members, friends, and colleagues.

Indeed, Thailand would be busting out all over.

The inaugural program was made available to the public in February, 2003. More than 100 women between the ages of sixteen and sixty enrolled. The participants were from all walks of life—professional women in business, beauticians, travel agents, tour guides, housewives, and students.

After reading about the Thai program, I decided to get some reaction. But first, I wondered if this was unique to Thailand. Had any other countries developed a similar program for their women?

"Good morning, this is the Embassy of Switzerland," a cheerful female voice said. "Can I help you?"

"May I speak to your public information officer?" I asked.

"What about, sir?"

"Perhaps I can explain the subject matter to the PIO."

"I need to know which department your inquiry will be directed to. That's why the subject is necessary, sir."

Stammering and stuttering, I said, "Ummm, er, female breasts are the subject matter. I blundered badly, despite my practice sessions before making the call.

"Pardon?"

Great—she didn't hang up. Here was my second chance. "I am researching a story about the Thai government sponsoring a program to build better breasts for its women. Thai women are dancing their way to better busts. I was wondering if the Swiss health authorities offer a similar program."

She giggled.

"The Thai government's program avoids costly surgery, and no foreign objects are introduced into a woman's body. And the training is free."

The Swiss Miss giggled again.

"Sir, I know the perfect person to answer your inquiry."

After a few moments, another woman, Zita Germanier, was on the line. I explained that I was writing a story for *Metro* magazine,

Bangkok's popular English-language monthly. She was informed about the nature of the free program.

She couldn't restrain from chortling. Was this too trivial for her to take seriously? "The only breasts that the Swiss government wants to enhance are cow's breasts," she said.

"Say that again, please. I caught the nuance but I forgot the exact wording." With pen ready, she repeated and I copied.

"By having bigger cow breasts, we can produce more milk to make cheese, as well as make more milk-chocolate to export."

"You're a wonder," I said.

"On a serious note," Zita said, "Switzerland doesn't have anything similar to the Thai government's program. I suppose that's why Thailand is known as 'Amazing Thailand.'"

Next stop: the Embassy of the United States.

After hearing my introductory remarks, a man said, "I'll connect you to the person who can help you."

The person turned out to be a woman. She took my e-mail address and told me that she would check the database of the US Public Health and Human Resources departments.

"Before I hang up," she said, "can I have some information about building a better bust?"

"Is your breast small or big?"

"Why do you ask?"

"There are programs to stop big breasts from sagging, or to make small breasts bigger."

"I want bigger ones. But please, don't use my name."

Next stop: Italy.

The Italian Embassy's information officer, a lady, upon hearing what the Thai government was doing, made this comment: "It's obvious that big bazooms are in vogue worldwide. But there is no such program sponsored by the Italian government."

She added that Nature had been kind to many Italian women. "But unfortunately, I am not one of them. How can I get information about the exercises?"

Like the lady in the US Embassy, I advised her to pick up the next issue of *Metro* and check out the exercises that would be presented in an easy-to-follow pictorial format.

Next stop: France.

Guy Heidelberger, a friend of mine, is the director of Alliance Française in Chiang Rai. He was intrigued by what the Thai government was doing for its women. "Sorry, but France has nothing like it," he said. "*Vivre* Thailand."

How about a Muslim country, I wondered. . . .

"Hello, Egyptian Embassy, Bangkok."

"Hello" I said, and introduced myself. "I am researching a story about the government of Thailand sponsoring a program to make better breasts for Thai women. I wonder if the Egyptian government has a similar program for the women of Egypt."

I expected scorn, derision, or to hear the phone slam. Instead, I was told to hold as the call was being transferred to the Commissioner's Office.

After a musical interlude of two minutes, a male voice said, "This is the Commissioner's Office. Am I to understand that the Thai government has a program to make better breasts for Thai women?"

"Your understanding is correct, commissioner."

Instead of mockery, there was laughter from the 'Commish.'

"Tell me more."

Details were provided: women cupping their breasts during the open-air exercise; shaking of breasts with quick movements from the waist, whence wiggling mammaries were in evidence.

Instead of being ticked, the 'Commish' was tickled.

"Only in Thailand could this happen," he said. After a pause, he continued, "Egypt is a Muslim country. Women must hide their breasts. In fact, it would be bad for men to see women's breasts, whether they are big or little."

Conceal, not reveal, was the policy.

Determined to get an answer, I asked, "Bad for men in what way, sir?"

"You know, men get excited easily."

Next stop: Laos, a small-breasted country bordering Thailand. "Nothing like it in Laos," the lady information officer said.

Now to Malaysia, another country bordering Thailand. And another Muslim country.

The female officer admitted that the Malaysian government had no such program. I asked if my perception was accurate—that Malay women, like their Thai sisters, were generally small-breasted.

"Not true. Malaysian breasts are bigger than Thai breasts." She did not invoke the Muslim decree to conceal, not reveal.

Next stop: Denmark.

The lady there expressed intrigue over the Thai program. "How funny," she said. "But we have nothing like it in Denmark."

How about a Latin country? I mused.

"Hello, Mexican Embassy."

"Good afternoon. I'm writing a feature story for *Metro* magazine."

"How can I help you, sir?"

"The Thai government has a program where women dance their way to better breasts. It's free. No cosmetic surgery is required."

The officer, another lady, said, "Unheard of. Nothing like it in the Republic of Mexico."

Two days later, I received an e-mail message from the American Embassy. An exhaustive search of the numerous agencies within the US public health system and the Department of Human Resources disclosed that there is no better-breast program in existence or even in the planning stage.

My friend Brenda Lee in Puerto Rico commented via e-mail: "No such helpful program here in Puerto Rico. If there had been, I wouldn't have spent 5,000 dollars for my breast reduction."

Continuing my research on the Internet, I found an interesting comment from a feminist and law professor, Malee Pruegpongsawalee: "Women are bombarded with nonsense by the advertising industry and beauty-care peddlers that they must be curvy and gifted with blooming breasts to be sexually desirable," she said in a report. "Those who don't fit the mold are made to feel inadequate; so much so that they're willing to put their body through all sorts of pain to feel beautiful."

Malee claimed that self-esteem should be based on personal competence, and rejected concepts of beauty that relegate women to being seen only as sex objects.

A male cosmetic surgeon who observed the first day of the training program held at the Institute of Thai Traditional Medicine, scoffed at the idea that breasts can be enhanced or reduced or made firmer by the exercise regimen. "It's impossible," he said. "It's like telling people they can go to Koh Samui from Bangkok by road. But we know a boat must be taken to the island." The surgeon requested anonymity.

Nata Oottapong, 27, had been attracted to the healing arts since her teens. After graduating from high school, she studied different massage techniques—herbal, aromatic, oil, and the traditional *rusi dai ton*, the yoga discipline taught at the Institute of Thai Traditional Medicine. Nata works at the posh Echo Valley Spa and Fitness Center in Bangkok. She also worked at the spa's headquarters in Vancouver, Canada, on a one-year assignment.

"I heard about the dance training program while I was studying *rusi dai ton* at the Institute," she said. "So I joined right away."

Nata was excited about developing bigger breasts. She exercised twenty minutes in the morning and another twenty minutes before bedtime.

As of this writing, Nata had been in breast training for three weeks. When asked about 'before and after' measurements to determine the method's effectiveness, Nata took her measurement only on the first day—"Thirty-one inches."

She was resisting the temptation to measure again until she completed the three-month training.

Not only did Nata expect to see evidence of "dream breasts," she was also excited about the prospect of "dream cleavage."

The least favorite part of the regimen occurs when "I splash my breasts with the bottle of cold water, especially in the morning. Brrrrrr."

When exercising, she purrs her favorite mantra—"We must, we must, increase our bust."

John Wayne Bobbitt
And The Bangkok Haircut

ON THE FATEFUL DAY of June 23, 1993, a man named John Wayne Bobbitt became front-page news throughout the United States and around the globe. The unexpected surgical action performed upon John Wayne by Lorena Bobbitt, his then-wife, was known as the "cut heard around the world." In a fit of rage, she sliced off a chunky portion of John Wayne's phallus with an eleven-inch kitchen knife. She claimed that she had been battered by husband Wayne. In revenge, she battered back. She also claimed that her husband left her "sexually unfulfilled." Her third accusation was John Wayne's promiscuity during their tumultuous three-year marriage.

To make sure that the misbehaving phallus would not be re-attached, Lorena Bobbitt drove to the outskirts of Manassas, Virginia, forty miles from Washington, D.C., and threw the despised object out the car window, into the shrubbery along the highway.

John Wayne Bobbitt was rushed to the hospital. He begged the police to locate the vital missing part of his anatomy. With dogged determination, the police scoured the countryside for the severed organ. Luckily, it was found before the crucial eleventh hour. If not attached before that time, the likelihood of successful re-uniting of the flesh diminishes.

A year after the 1993 assault, Lorena Bobbitt went on trial. When CNN cut away from the court proceedings to focus on then-President Clinton's visit to Kiev in the Ukraine, outraged viewers bombarded CNN headquarters in Atlanta, Georgia with complaints. Courtroom interruptus was out of the question. Marital affairs contained more drama than international affairs. As a result, CNN was pressured into going back to court. The news channel no longer disappointed its American and worldwide audience during the sensational two-week trial.

The jury learned why Lorena Bobbitt was driven to perform her drastic deed. During her marriage, she was subjected to repeated physical and mental cruelty and 'rape.' One witness for the defense reported that John Wayne boasted that he "threw her bodily," "pushed her," "shoved her," and "tried to hit her with any object he could find." Eleven other witnesses for the defense testified that they were present when John Wayne "beat and humiliated his wife in public."

A psychiatrist for the defense pointed out that, by emasculating her husband, Lorena made him feel as powerless as she had been. It was a reap-what-you-sow explanation. The fruits of karmic action resulted in a karmic reaction. The boomerang effect.

The battered wife syndrome won the hearts and minds of the jurors. After a short deliberation, the defendant, Lorena Bobbitt, was found not guilty by reason of what was called an "irresistible impulse"— another term for temporary insanity and diminished capacity.

◆

In his detective thriller, *Bangkok Tattoo*, published in 2005, John Burdett, a barrister turned novelist, opens the story this way:

> *The bar girl is dressed in silk, so skimpy it barely manages to cover nipples and butt. Not that anyone notices, since she's soaked in blood, raving about farangs and off her skull on opium in a cheap hotel in Soi Cowboy, Bangkok's notorious red light district.*
>
> *On the floor lies the body of an American spy, her former lover. On the table, his severed penis.*

The prestigious *American Journal Of Surgery* views Thailand as the foremost country in the world with the expertise to re-unite a severed phallus to its owner. While the United States has seen only two incidents of the "cut heard around the world," Thailand has witnessed at least 100 reported cases since 1978. During that same span of time, Canada and Australia recorded only one incident each, while Sweden experienced three phallus separations. Thailand leads the world in both detachment and re-attachment.

What wife Lorena did to husband John Wayne is known in Thailand as the "Bangkok haircut." The American medical journal pointed out that the Thai woman's penchant for dealing with wayward husbands or boyfriends has also worked its way into popular parlance as "feeding the ducks"—after a notorious case in the kingdom in which an irate wife fed her husband's pecker to the ducks on their farm.

Some Thai women boil the male organ in water, taking joy that it will not be re-united. Others secure the hacked phallus to a helium balloon and watch the despised organ float to kingdom come. Flushing the critter down the toilet is another popular method of disposal.

The leading Thai specialist in restoring the male member is Dr. Surasak Muangsombot. He works in one of Thailand's best hospitals, Paolo Memorial, in Bangkok, which specializes in surgical re-attachment of severed schlongs.

Dr. Surasak and his surgical team have reunited the phallus to 33 victims since 1978. I thought the good doctor would be a good man to talk to. I called, and the noted surgeon agreed to answer questions in a telephone interview.

"Dr. Surasak, are you still at re-attachment number 33?"

"Two months ago I re-attached the thirty-fourth penis to its owner."

He pointed out that the true number of cases could be closer to 1,000, perhaps even more. The Thai 'tradition' has become so widespread that doctors have had to come up with imaginative and creative techniques to persuade wives and girlfriends—who want to prevent re-attachment—to divulge the whereabouts of the severed items.

Dr. Surasak's most difficult case was caused by an angry wife who had to be bribed to tell of the phallus's new location. She had thrown it into a septic tank. A wrecking crew was assembled to retrieve it.

"I asked the nurse to clean it up," Dr. Surasak said, "and warned the patient that he may get septicemia. The victim said, 'Do your best, and if it gets septicemia, I will die with my penis.'"

The surgeon added that "it was fifteen hours between it being chopped off and re-attached, which is much longer than the books say it can be done, but, at the pleading of the patient, our team went ahead. To our surprise and delight, everything went fine."

While the success rate of re-attaching the phallus is "one hundred percent," Dr. Surasak thinks that only about half that number can again experience the previous level of phallus functioning.

"So far, there has not been a single documented case of a new baby. Out of the 34 cases I've done, I don't think that any can sustain a prolonged erection. That makes it difficult to make a new baby."

"How did you get started in re-attaching severed phalluses?"

"My previous experience in re-attaching appendages was an amputated finger."

"Then in 1978 you had your first case of—"

"Yes, it was in 1978."

"How many students have you trained in this kind of surgery?"

"Fifty-six. They are practicing throughout the kingdom, including government hospitals."

"What about the cost involved?"

"Two hundred thousand baht—or five thousand US dollars. It includes hospitalization, medication, surgery, and follow-up care."

"What!" I was incredulous. "I thought it would be 20,000 US. Maybe more."

"You must remember that Thai people are poor."

"What about men who can't afford the 200,000? Can they get the treatment with the 'Thirty Baht Plan'?"

"All hospitals subscribing to the Plan must provide the necessary services to the unfortunate victim. If the hospital is not equipped, the person is transferred to another hospital."

"How many of the victims have been *farang*?"

"To my knowledge, none."

"I thought that many would have been *farang*."

"Thai women are smart. They don't want to cut off their bankroll. They realize that *farangs* are well-endowed financially."

"Someone told me that a German in Pattaya had his phallus sliced off by his girlfriend about a year ago. The enraged woman, I was told, had her cheating boyfriend take her to his favorite German restaurant, where they enjoyed their favorite dishes. They drank two good bottles of German wine, went home, and had good sex. After the cutting, she fed the phallus to the duck."

"Did you hear that story in a bar?"

"Hmmm, yes."

"A good bar story."

"Has anyone ever had the experience of *two* 'Bangkok haircuts'?"

Dr. Surasak laughed. "That would amount to being struck by lighting twice. That would make him a real loser. So far, no repeat customers."

◆

Doctors, psychologists, and social commentators claim that the slashing epidemic is due to a combination of factors. Polygamy was common practice in Thailand until it was banned a century ago, but it still persists, and the phallus—in Hinduism and animism (both of which have a powerful influence in Thai spirituality)—is revered as a symbol of power and fertility. (Only in Thailand has Mother Nature carved a statue of rock that has a striking resemblance to the phallus. The rock is on the island of Koh Samui, and is a popular tourist attraction for both Thai and foreign tourists. Mother Nature has also carved the female sex organ into the same rock formation, close to the male member. They are known as 'Grandfather' and 'Grandmother' by the local folk). Carved wooden and stone phalluses are found everywhere in the kingdom—in shops, on ships' prows, and in the rock gardens and shrines of big hotels, condos, and office buildings.

Thailand tries to emulate the West, where the practice is one man, one wife. But Thai psychologist and media commentator, Dr. Wallop Pryamanotham, agrees that the Bangkok haircut stems from the outlawed but flourishing Thai habit of keeping secret wives.

"In those bygone days," the psychologist said in a newspaper article, "a man could have many wives." Despite the ban, men still act the same way, keeping second wives and mistresses—known as *mia noi* ('minor wife'). One method of revenge is for the woman to take extreme measures. According to the doc, "The women are saying, 'If he won't have sex with me, I'll make sure he can't have it with other women.'"

Dr. Wallop added: "The symbol of potency is cut off. His power is gone." Apparently, this is revenge of the most meaningful kind.

Back in the USA, an enterprising woman in Oklahoma cashed in on the member mutilation scandal. Samantha Cudek, the manager of a pet supply shop in Tulsa, decided to call her new dog-chew product the "Bobbitt Jerky." The name recognition translated the item into hot sales. Through word-of-mouth, customers she had never seen before flocked to her store. Samantha increased her sales ten-fold, then twenty-fold. "Dogs love bones," she intoned, "especially a Bobbitt bone." The news resounded through Tulsa and beyond.

Samantha Cudek became an instant celeb. During radio talk show interviews, she delighted her hosts with quips like, "We know the power of a bull. Our Bobbitt bone is made from a bull's penis."

Another Samantha quip: "Your dog's stamina will increase with the Bobbitt bone because it's made from a Nature-made body part."

"The Bobbitt bone is a foot-long beef stick," Samantha said. She also claimed that the dog chew was good for teething puppies.

The product is indeed made from a bull's phallus.

Even staid scientists have succumbed to the Bobbitt hoopla. The following is taken from the respected Internet site, Wikipedia:

> *Eunice aphroditois . . . is an aquatic predatory polychaete worm dwelling at the ocean floor at depths of approximately 10-40 meters.*
>
> *This organism buries its long body into an ocean bed composed of gravel, mud or corals, where it waits patiently for outside stimulus to reach one of its five antennae. Armed with sharp claws, it is known to attack with such speeds that its prey is sometimes sliced in half. Although the worm hunts for food, it is omnivorous.*

Little is known about the sexual habits and life span of this worm, but researchers hypothesize that sexual reproduction occurs at an early stage. . . .

The female may attack the male's sex organ after mating, detaching it with her sharp bone plates and then feeding it to her young.

These creatures can grow to nearly three meters and are thought to have a very long life span.

The common name applied by marine biologists is "Bobbitt worm."

"Sex And The City" Goes Thai

WE AT *METRO* magazine were determined to find out why Thailand thrives on HBO's chic chick show, "Sex And The City." What is it about the men and women in the series? HBO's female characters can be viewed as voluptuous vixens, as thirty-something New York desperados (desperate for men) who are seen as dramatic losers or cunning survivors.

It's obvious that men (both Thai and foreign) watch the show because they are privy to girl talk. Men can peer into the mysteries of the female mind, taking delight as the feminine mystique unravels on a weekly basis.

But do Thai women, like their counterparts in New York, treat their men like sex objects? Do Thai women make outrageous remarks on their first date; quips like: "I have an itch that I hope you can help me out with?" Has "Sex And The City" resulted in a clash between conservative Thai traditions and brash Western openness? To answer these and other concerns, I was dispatched to probe the minds of four women who participated in a special investigation into the female mind. (We are grateful to HBO for providing some of the multiple-choice questions posted on their website.)

For "Sex And The City Goes Thai" we take this opportunity to introduce the four women who volunteered to be probed.

The first was Kham Phaka, (Golden Flower in Thai). This is her pen name. In Lanna slang, which is rich in irony, Kham Phaka also translates as Loose Woman. A controversial figure, she challenges traditional Thai values by constantly "shouting from the rooftop" that she is a *dokthong* ['slut']." In other circles, including *Metro*, she is given the revered sobriquet of "Nude Scholar" (and is the Thai equivalent of Carrie).

Kham Phaka is a doctoral candidate at Kyoto University in Japan. She is a prolific writer, the author of six non-fiction books on sex-gender issues and relationships. Her best-known work is *Krathoo Dokthong (Slut Agenda)*. Her Ph.D. dissertation was based in part on *Slut Agenda*. The academic title of her dissertation is "The History Of Sexuality And Nationalism As Portrayed In Thai Romance Novels From 1880 To 1930."

The Nude Scholar writes weekly columns for two Thai newspapers and three Thai monthly magazines. According to a full-page feature story in *The Nation* (October 24, 2004), her critics see this 32-year-old social commentator as "a woman who violates Thai morals, cultural

49

beliefs, and traditions." She added fuel to her critics' fires by posing in the nude—a Thai taboo—for *GM Plus*.

Another faithful viewer of the popular HBO series is Julie Kaufman, 33, a DJ on Bangkok's 102.5 FM radio. She is the Thai equivalent of Miranda, the serious one. Her mother is Thai and her father American. Raised in the United States and the UK, Julie calls Bangkok her home. Being a *luk krueng* (Thai and Western, or Eurasian), she provides an unusual perspective from her *farang* and Thai cultural heritage. She is married to a Brit and has a baby girl named Sara. During her radio gig, Julie's listeners call in to discuss a variety of topics.

The third viewer of "Sex And The City," Georgia Rachatawet, is the Thai version of Sweet Charlotte. Aged 26, she was born and raised in Bangkok. "I totally Thai," she said, obviously proud of her origin. A blues and jazz singer with charisma galore and a flair for comedy, Georgia and her band perform at a variety of venues around Bangkok. After a spicy rendition of a song, in a demure tone, she joshes the audience, "How many had orgasm?" She recalls a Western woman approaching her during a break: "*Farang* lady say to me, 'You made me wet.'"

The fourth and final woman is the Thai version of Samantha. In her mid-thirties, she agreed to participate in the study providing that her identity be withheld. 'Samantha' is well known in fashion and television circles. A *bon vivant*, she is immediately recognized when she makes an entrance into glitzy nightspots in Bangkok, Singapore, Hong Kong, and Paris. The elusive celeb has evaded the paparazzi for the past two years. The extraordinary feat of frustrating the press is due partly to the creation of her network of counter-paparazzi spies. She has not been captured in a compromising situation since setting up her intelligence cadre.

◆

In one episode of the show, the TV Samantha found out that her boyfriend was two-timing her. Determined to expose him as a cheat, she made up flyers and posted them on lampposts in the section of Manhattan where he worked.

A policewoman told her it was against the law to deface public property with signs.

To which Samantha replied: "I caught my boyfriend eating another woman's sushi."

To which the policewoman replied: "Go ahead, ma'am."

I asked the ladies the same first question: *What would you do if you caught your boyfriend eating another woman's sushi?*

Nude Scholar (Carrie): If he is a serious boyfriend, we need to talk. But if he is not, he has the right to try other kinds of sushi.

Julie (Miranda): I saw that shocking episode and was totally disgusted! I couldn't believe they showed it on TV. But I guess that's HBO. I don't think any real Thai woman would give you an answer to this tough question, but I am half Thai and half American. I am happily married and we have a beautiful baby girl. I don't think my husband would ever be in that situation. He still believes in monogamy—one of the very few men who still believes in it . . . thank God! I felt sorry for Samantha. She was shocked, as I would be—and I would no longer date that man—but she was so desperate and she really loved that creep. So if that was me, the guy would be history. But I don't think I would be with a man like that anyway. I really believe in trust and friendship first and foremost in a relationship.

Georgia (Charlotte): I be upset if I am in the situation like this, but I wouldn't do anything to the guy. I think I let him do what he wants, but I'd have to leave him because if I have to be with somebody I can't trust—that is not really a relationship. That will be very hard for me to decide, but I also could give him a chance to change, too.

Samantha: That's a hard question. I haven't had any of my lovers cheating on me as far as I know. I don't think I would care that much if he did. If he wants to do it with someone else, go ahead. I'm not going to be vindictive or anything like that. Some Thai women may want to cut off their lovers' private and feed it to the ducks, but that kind of retaliation doesn't appeal to me.

Men are curious to know a woman's answer to this one. How important is the size of a man's sushi tickler to you? Is the diameter also important?

Nude Scholar: For me it is very important. It does make a difference, really. Bigger is better, because inside me the feeling is different. And it's fun to touch something that's powerful.

Julie: What's important is what he does with what he has.

Georgia: All sizes fit me. [She chuckles]. I am okay with the size the man sport. I like small guys, skinny build. On the other hand, it all depends on how he uses what he has. If they know the way to keep me aroused, I'm thrilled.

Samantha: For me, size doesn't really matter much. I like it between 5-6.5 inches. It's the hardness and the action that I care about. Many *farangs* are better endowed than Thai men. Sometimes it can be too big for a small girl like me. Personally, I prefer a fatter beef than a long, thin one. When it's too long, it hurts the inside of my pussy after a long intercourse. The action is very important to me. The guy has to be passionate and hot and show me that I'm wanted. I have to be stimulated and fully aroused before he puts it in. When I'm ready, I forget about the size.

What are your thoughts about having sex with a virgin guy?

Nude Scholar: It's fine. Why not? We will learn and hopefully will discover a new world together.

Georgia: Why not? If a virgin and me connect through conversation and there's romance in the air, I'm all for de-flowering him.

Julie: I hope he is my husband firstly, and if he is, then great. I hope he enjoys every moment of it. I'm sure he would.

Samantha: I've had at least three virgin guys so far. It's kind of fun when I learn that he has never done it. I get a chance to show him and teach him things. A drawback is they always explode in a few minutes. I decided that three virgins is enough for me. I no longer desire to have sex with virgins, because I don't want to waste time in the role of a teacher. Rolling in the hay with experienced and confident guys is now more satisfying.

Samantha is having lunch with her girlfriend, and the girlfriend's date. When another man joins them in the booth, Samantha makes her intentions known that she is going to have him for lunch. She ducks under the table and blows him away. Nude Scholar, have you ever done anything as spontaneous and uninhibited as this? If so, please elaborate

Nude Scholar: Well, I have never done anything like that. It is too cool for me. Sometimes I want to walk up to a guy who excites me. I think of saying, "I want to fuck you." Many times the guy picks up my feeling, because he asks me first.

Julie: Ditto for me. In my younger days, I did something spontaneous, but I'm not going to elaborate.

Georgia: I'm Sweet Charlotte. I could never be as daring as Samantha. She's a hot babe. Ready all the time, even in a public place, although she tries to hide under a table. But that's still public sex.

Samantha: I did it a couple times on VIP bus tours to Chiang Mai and Khon Kaen. In both situations, I was sitting two rows from the back with my boyfriend. There were just a few people behind us. I'm sure that they knew what was going on. When I was a university student, I had sex with my college boyfriends in the woods on an undeveloped area of the campus. I learned later that there were groups of observers that would come out and see live shows there. If they were there, I'm sure they must have seen me.

Speaking of sex in public, that will be coming up soon. This is Samantha's advice to Carrie: "Go out and have sex. Just like a man. Treat men as sex objects." Do you think it would be fun to be as free and easy as Samantha about having casual sex and treating men as sex objects?

Nude Scholar: I don't think so. I said in the interview with *GM Plus* that, between having casual sex and being at home masturbating, I prefer masturbation because it is just about the orgasm. So why should I have to shave my legs, do the make-up thing, fix my hair, get a good dress, have dinner etcetera, and more, just for an orgasm that I can do by myself. Plus, casual sex might not be enjoyment if the guy is not good in bed.

What about you, Julie? You're in the unusual position of having a perspective from both cultural sides.

Nude Scholar: Just a minute, please. I'm not finished.

Sorry, please continue.

Nude Scholar: I love having intimate sex, not just meaningless fucking. I don't think that being just like a man is good for women. It's not progressive, nor is it empowering to women. My question is, "Why be like men?" We must realize that femininity and masculinity are social constructions. Our aim should not be to be equal to them. We are defined by our social history. Our work is not to compete and try to be the same or equal. I don't want to be 'just like a man.' We women have to wake the men up and ask them, "Hey, are you happy about working hard to support the whole family? Are you happy about not being able to cry? Do you feel lonely after fucking and on a one-night stand? Are you tired with trying to be a damn good, warm, caring father? Why do you put pictures of your loving wife and children in your office? Are you trying to show that you are being respectful to your family? Or because you really love them? Come on, tell me that sometimes you get deadly bored with your wife.

Julie? You have a perspective from both sides.

Julie: I think Thai women are just like *farang* women, but they hide it better. Women are women, no matter what culture they are in. Some are more suppressed by society. But there are things hidden and unseen in all societies, if you know what I mean.

Georgia: Nude Scholar, Julie, and the Thai Samantha are more beautiful than me. I haven't seen Samantha, but from her job in fashion and TV, I imagine she must be a knockout. I bet she and the other two get hit on for casual sex. Never happen to me. Make me cry. [After a brief sob, she wipes her eyes]. About treating men like sex objects: I think it very good idea.

Samantha: Umm, I forgot the question.

The American Samantha has stated again and again that she loves to treat men as sex objects. Do you agree with her?

Samantha: An emphatic YES. It's okay to treat men as sex objects as long as you are not serious about them in the relationship. You can enjoy them as much as you want. Thai men do that with their mistresses and prostitutes all the time. If they can afford it, I would say eighty percent of them would do it behind their wives' backs. There are so many outlets available for men in Thailand. Now that Thai society is more open, it's a good time for a woman to be free and easy as she wishes. Even though I'm free and easy, because of AIDS I'm still extremely careful with guys. I don't trust them, so I always use condoms and carry some in my purse in case of emergency.

Before answering the next question, here is an update on alleged explicit sexual behavior by Thai teens on public transportation. The Bangkok Mass Transit Authority came under fire from commuters in August 2004 after the news media ran a series of stories about the indecent behavior of students on public buses, in fast-food restaurants, and in shopping centers. [The Nation.] The exposé highlighted kissing, embracing, and intimate fondling. The college students are particularly fond of using the air-con buses with curtained windows.

"I have interviewed bus conductors and some passengers, and they confirm that students are having sex, especially on the air-con bus route 12," said Virat Chokkatiwat, a director of the BMTA.

Bus route 12 travels past two of Bangkok's universities, and completes its journey on the outskirts of the capital. Students refer to their public displays as nothing more than "making out." It has been reported that "going all the way" is part of making out. This is popular in the evening hours, when it is dark.

To put an end to the practice, route 12 posted notices that say: "Thai women should preserve old culture about sexual behavior."

The Education Ministry takes a dismal view of the problem. According to The Nation (Sept 6, 2004), the Ministry is "determined to end the lewd and obscene public behavior of some students. A plan to draft a regulation is on the table. Tossaport Sererak, secretary to the education minister, claims the regulation will instill the offenders with a 'sense of decency.'"

Sex on buses and in fast-food restaurants and shopping centers? Do you see a relationship between Thai youth engaging in sex acts in public places and the influence of "Sex And The City"?

Nude Scholar: With Western influence or not, with "Sex And The City" or not, Thais youths and adults have been fucking, selling sex, having mistresses, practicing infidelity, in many ways. Thai people like being gay, being lesbian, being bi. In Thai history we like to fuck the dogs and the cows and the water buffalo.

Sex is everywhere. So I'm not surprised to know that there are boys and girls having sex on a bus. And what's the difference between having sex on the bus or in a hotel or in their bedroom? This news gives us the implication that as long as they don't do it in public, it's fine. If there is anything I am worried about, I worry that in Thai society we are so hypocritical when it comes to sex. Plus, when we are talking about sex, it means fucking. We have never put sex in the political or historical context. When we think about sex, we don't question sexuality, gender. We cannot see the connection between sex and the State. Why does the State want to legislate about sex? Why is sex among the youth wrong nowadays when, in the past, people had kids when they were twelve or thirteen years old? You can discuss these issues without concerning the role of the modern nation State.

Julie: Ummm. I haven't seen this and I really don't want to either. Have you seen it? I think it's gross and probably very uncomfortable and very messy.

Yes, we would like to see where and how it's done. But it's too late. The route 12 bus has removed the curtains from the windows. There are special patrols on the bus to prevent any public display of sexual activity.

Georgia: Ohhh, my god. Sex on the bus. Sex in malls. Sex in fast-food shops. You joking, yes?

Not joking. It's really happened. Then patrols were put on the bus and the curtains removed from the windows.

Georgia: Bangkok is more hot than New York. Another reason for me not to stay in New York.

Samantha: I already talked about my sexual experience in public, when I was a student almost twenty years ago. I admit that I was quite brave to do it then. To answer your question, I don't think it's influenced by "Sex And The City." It's a combination of many things: sexy Hollywood movies, porno movies, availability of cheap short-time hotels, and all kinds of media. That, I think, is happening all over the world.

How do you explain the incredible popularity of "Sex And The City." in the Land of Smiles?

Nude Scholar: It is a contemporary fairy tale. Cinderella in our generation can have multiple orgasms with many guys before she meets the prince.

Julie: I think people like the fashion and style of the girls on the show. They are so hip. Bangkok is a hip city.

Georgia: "Sex And The City" is very shocking to Thai people. We used to be traditional in our ways. Now we more like *farang.*

Samantha: I love this show. I knew right away that I was Samantha. Now I don't feel too guilty to be a horny Thai woman, because I'm sure that there are girls like me everywhere. Thai men also love this show because it's fun to watch and learn about the sex lives of white American women, how women talk to each other, how people live in New York City.

What is it about the show that appeals to each of you?

Nude Scholar: Carrie's shoes. I wonder if a columnist in New York can really afford all those expensive shoes and be so stylish in her fashion.

Julie: I love the individual characters. And I miss New York. I grew up in Connecticut, about a 45-minute drive to New York. We went to 'the City' on many weekends. I love the dialogue between the girls. I also love the fact that they are not so young and that they are not too thin or too perfect. In that way, it's almost like real life, but a bit exaggerated.

Georgia: The show all about sexy women, sexy dress, sexy city, sexy talk, sexy boyfriends, sexy ex-boyfriends. In this way, New York and Bangkok same-same.

Samantha: It's the characters in the show. I really enjoy watching Samantha, because she is my soul sister. I am not as promiscuous as she is, because I'm afraid of AIDS, and it's harder for me to find guys that I'm attracted to sexually. I like white men, but most of my colleagues are Thai. The show is also realistic and too much fun not to watch.

What do you feel is more important to Samantha? A) being at peace spiritually; B) a perfect marriage; C) a successful career; D) multiple orgasms? Before answering, keep in mind this statement from Samantha: "Last night I could not stop thinking about a Big Mac. I finally had to get dressed, go out, and pick up a guy."

Nude Scholar: That's easy—a perfect marriage and multiple orgasms with her lovers.

Julie: What do you think? Samantha is not a normal woman! She is a nymphomaniac. But I think that deep down, way deep down, she wants to find that perfect someone to love her and marry her. For me it would be being at peace spiritually. Then my marriage and family. There is no such thing as a perfect marriage. There is no perfect anything, really.

Georgia: Very easy to answer. Orgasm every day sooooo important to Samantha. She need sex more than air. She like 'big O' all the time.

You want to hear my saying? My saying: "Hit my *pooh-see* with your rhythm stick."

Samantha: Here is my answer in order of importance: D, A, C, B. I want to respond to the Thai Miranda's remark that the American Samantha is not a normal person. She is, to quote Julie, "a nymphomaniac." True.

I also want to respond to Julie's comment that, deep down, Samantha wants "to find that perfect someone to love and marry her." That's true, but it's also true that I can feel complete without having a man in my life. I know that's a contradiction.

Do you need someone who can keep up? What is the ideal age of a man that you prefer to date? A) someone close to your own age; B) someone a little older than you; C) younger guys?

Nude Scholar: Any age.

Julie: Someone close to my age.

Samantha: I want somebody who can keep up with me. Age doesn't really matter, as long as he is not too old, as long as we look good together while walking on the street. I don't want to date guys that are ten years younger either. I need to be able to converse with him. The guy has to be sophisticated enough to know what I'm talking about and he must be compatible with me in lots of other ways. He has to be smart, strong, sexy, not boring. Most importantly, our sex has to be really good in order for me to keep the relationship with him.

Georgia: What it mean, "keep up"?

We explain.

Georgia: *He he he.* I choose none of above. Age not important to me. Depends on the guy. "Keep up." I like it when he "keep up." Make me happy.

Miracle Milk

ACCORDING TO A PROGRAM on the Discovery Channel, the female polar bear produces the richest milk of any mammal. The polar bear observation may be true, but it is my belief that only the human female can produce milk that results in the healing of physical, emotional, mental, and spiritual problems.

John Steinbeck, in his novel *The Grapes Of Wrath*, also believed in the magical and mysterious properties of woman. After giving birth to a stillborn baby, a distraught woman cradled the dead child in her arms. Her own mother then told her that a man in the migrant workers' camp nearby was very weak and could not digest food. He was dying of starvation. The mother pleaded for her daughter to breast-feed the emaciated man. Hospitalization and tube feeding were not options for the underpaid migrant workers in Steinbeck's classic about the Depression days. The distraught woman realized she had the power to save the dying man. She breast-fed him.

Pira Sudham, the Thai novelist who was nominated for the Nobel Prize for *Siamese Drama*—a short story about life in the sun-scorched paddy fields of Isaan (where the average annual income for a farming family of four is 500 US dollars)—gives us this brief but haunting account of a woman's power: "She sings her children to sleep. She is like the earth and the skies."

Many other novels, films, and stage plays depict scenes of men dying on battlefields. Their last words are invariably about their mother. Not only has the female nurtured them as children, the dying men have a vision in their mind's eye of a female comforting them in death.

The power of a woman—magical, mysterious, miraculous.

In June, 2004, I heard from a Thai friend an amazing story about a Thai grandmother who produces breast milk that is believed to possess magical, healing power. Pissamai Trapsukhorn is a well-known *mor doo*, or 'fortune-teller.' She lives and practices her craft in Bangkok. She was 72 years of age. Apparently her milk is supernatural—it is said to ease pain, heal paralysis, and cure mental illness and other ailments.

In Thailand, Pissamai is viewed as a fortune-teller. The literal translation of the Thai word *mor doo* is 'doctor who sees'—where 'seeing' is through the sixth sense. In the West—where female psychics and healers outnumber their male counterparts by a staggering ratio of eighty percent to twenty percent—Pissamai might be known as a psychic healer who also possesses additional powers of clairvoyance and mental telepathy.

I did some Internet research. A newspaper article in the *Thai Post* quoted a doctor at Chulalongkorn University, Thailand's most prestigious medical school. He stated that, "Mammary glands usually stop producing milk two or three years after childbirth. Most women stop lactating in their forties." The physician continued: "A lactating woman at age 72 must have unusual hormones. She is a medical anomaly."

The article also stated that Pissamai claimed she was a fallen angel who "plummeted to earth as punishment for having casual sex with another deity."

I phoned Chocolate, my teacher and interpreter, and asked if she had heard about the old woman who was alleged to produce milk that heals.

"Do you mean Pissamai Trapsukhorn?" she asked.

Chocolate had read about her in the Thai newspapers and seen her interviewed on Thai TV.

I asked if arrangements could be made for an interview with the psychic healer.

Chocolate was successful and, a week later, a taxi swooshed us to a stately mansion in a remote section of Bangkok. From the lavish furnishings, including wooden carvings of Lord Buddha and other deities, it was obvious that the woman with the magical breasts had many and prosperous clients seeking her help.

We were shown into her 'healing room.' Pissamai was sitting on the floor in the lotus position. We smiled and exchanged greetings, and before I could say anything, she asked, "Do you have a Thai girlfriend?"

Instead of waiting for my reply, she said, "Not have Thai girlfriend, right?"

"Right, but I'm looking for one." It was true. At that time I hadn't met Lek, my current Thai girlfriend.

"Your problem," she said, "you focus too much on writing. Not enough time for a woman in your life. You want a romantic relationship and a wife, right?"

"Right on," I said.

Thinking that the interview was ready to get rolling, I was about to ask my first question. She waved her hand, signifying that she wasn't through.

"I must tell you things about your life. You tell me if I am right or wrong. I start with this—you had a bad back problem many years ago."

That's when it occurred to me that she had her *own* agenda.

Pissamai had peered into my past.

When I was twelve, I was in a body cast that went from my hips to the top of my chest. The condition hospitalized me for one year. My back malady was caused after an accident in a dumb game we played on the streets of Manhattan's Lower East Side.

"But your back not bother you anymore, right?"

I nodded. I didn't need any more convincing that she had clairvoyant powers.

She gave me a knowing smile. Her eyes had an eternal gaze.

"You must also be careful of your kidneys," she said.

Her comment stunned me. I listened as she told me, through Chocolate, that I had also suffered a serious kidney problem. Very true. The problem had been healed in Bangkok two years before, through a non-traditional medical approach known as the Buteyko Method—a drug-free breathing technique that has enabled thousands of people to reverse a wide range of chronic health problems by changing the way they breathe.

Pissamai warned me that to prevent a recurrence, I had to forsake excessive coffee intake and cut back on beer drinking with my buddies.

Once again, she was, to use the beatnik term, 'right on.' Surely, I thought, now the interview could begin.

Not so fast.

Having finished telling me about my relationship with women and past medical maladies, Pissamai then began to focus on my writing life. In my numerous interviews, I had always set the tempo, meaning that I was able to get the interviewee to focus on himself or herself. In my two meetings with Charles Manson in the California prison nuthouse, the psychopathic killer was a tame subject when compared to Pissamai. Manson concentrated on the questions.

"You are better known in Thailand than in the United States," Pissamai said.

Right on again.

"You have trouble getting paid by the magazines in Thailand."

True again.

"Through your writing about Thailand and Thai culture, you will become known in both countries."

I asked when that prophecy would come about.

"Before the end of the year 2004."

Very good. She gave me a definite date. She had been accurate in seeing my past and some happenings in the present. So, within six months, I would be able to confirm if she was accurate in seeing my future. I thanked her for the prophecy and said, "Let the interview begin."

Not so fast.

She took a blue chalk and began making circles on my bare right foot. Chocolate told me that this was her modus operandi. Instead of reading the hand, foot reading was her specialty. This was followed by a request for me to lie on her back.

While being sprawled out on this woman's back, she jostled me around, probably jingling more information. After five minutes of being tumbled and tossed, she indicated I get off the 'healing express.' Chocolate said that this procedure was done to transfer energy to me. In her words, I now "possessed more power."

Pissamai then said that she was prepared to give me her milk. She pushed up her blouse and revealed massive breasts that she was obviously proud of. She squeezed the nipple of her right breast and a milky liquid gushed forth. She had me kneel in front of her. She anointed my forehead as she intoned sacred chants in what I thought was the Pali language. As the milk touched my skin, I felt a tingling sensation winding its way inside my head. Rather than panicking from this bizarre occurrence, it dawned on me that feelings of warmth were taking place. She made me feel calm and safe in this nurturing atmosphere.

This ritual over, Pissamai announced that she had two important things to tell me. First, I would never get a disease. Second, I would never die.

Regarding her second announcement that I would never die, I have always felt that humans are designed to live in the same body for hundreds, no, thousands of years. Human cells are reborn and the body is renewed every five to seven years. Disease and infirmities are abnormal aberrations. Through cultural hypnosis and societal conditioning, our minds are instilled with the idea that we are terminal cases. But when bored with our earthly existence, we can make a conscious decision to take our body on a trip to other dimensions. That's what the 'Gentleman from Nazareth' did. He took a page from his predecessors, Enoch, Moses, and his sister Miriam. There are other biblical figures that took their physical bodies to the 'Ever Ever Land.' One of them is Elijah.

To my amazement, Pissamai had again tapped into my deep unconscious and plucked out my emotional belief that there might be no death if we discard the believe that preaches doomsday mortality.

With her eternal gaze, Pissamai saw my astonishment. She knew that she had penetrated the depths of my being.

At last it was time for the interview to begin.

Pissamai told me she has six children: four girls and two boys. Their ages ranged from 23 to 47. In true Thai tradition, three generations lived under the one roof.

I mentioned news reports that her clients drank her breast milk. The ritual she had performed on me only involved anointing my forehead.

"The media is wrong about clients drinking my supernatural milk," she replied.

I asked about her sexual affair with a deity when she was an angel, and she explained that she was kicked out of heaven for engaging in sex.

"Kicked out by whom?"

"The boss."

She was reluctant to elaborate on the forbidden liaison, except to point out that she was happy to return to earth, where she had unfinished business to take care of—the *mor doo* business of healing and gazing into peoples' thoughts.

"Did you have formal training in the healing arts?" I asked her.

She said that she studied under a master who told her that she had supernatural milk. She pointed to a picture of a man with cascading white hair. As a result of her mentor's advice, Pissamai has been practicing the milk of human kindness since she was fifty years old. She showed me three ledgers that contained the names of people she has worked with. During that time, she has traveled to the USA, Hong Kong, Singapore, and Australia, attending to people in distress.

I enquired about her husband, and Pissamai led Chocolate and me to one of the other rooms in the big house. Lying on a bed was an elderly man. His body was wasted. His fingers and toes were curled up, lifeless. Feeding tubes were attached to his scrawny arm. The man in a coma was her husband. Six months before, a second major stroke had left him in this debilitated condition.

"Why don't you heal him?" I asked.

She explained that his condition resulted from many years of smoking and drinking the deadly Mekhong 'whiskey' (actually a lethal kind of rum made from sugar cane). She said that his suffering was a result of action-reaction. The bad fruit of karma. The boomerang effect of his excesses.

Pissamai claimed that the "Angel of Death"—the Grim Reaper—hovered over her husband's bed. She said that she sees the Angel and that twelve others in the house had seen it, too. But Pissamai said that she had an ongoing dialog with the "Death Catcher," who had wanted to whisk her husband away shortly after the stroke. She had pleaded that her husband be allowed to continue his suffering for an extended period.

"Do you want to keep your husband alive because you hate him?" I asked.

"It's not a matter of hatred, but of love," she retorted.

By suffering in this life, he was making merit, whether he was conscious or in a coma. Through his daily suffering, deposits were made into his spiritual bank account. When his time to depart came, it would be payback time, meaning his new port of entry would be joyous.

◆

Pissamai's prophecy about my writing came true, but she was a year off the mark. On December 5th, 2005, I received an e-mail from Paiboon Publishing. The company expressed interest in my book proposal and asked for my phone number. Two days later, they phoned me from Berkeley, California to discuss the project. The book is now in your hands.

For centuries novelists, poets, and scientists alike have pondered the potency of human breast milk in curing sicknesses of the mind and body. We know that a woman's milk provides nourishment for a newborn. At the same time, it can contain enough nourishment to save the life of a dying man. In Thailand, Pissamai Trapsukhorn, this septuagenarian grandmother, remains a mystery to the established medical community. Not only does she continue to lactate in the seventh decade of her life, her "divine nectar" has the power to heal.

The Forrest Gump Of Thailand

WHEN I INTRODUCED the idea of writing about Atip (pronounced 'Ahh-tip') Muangsuwan as Thailand's version of the movie hero, Forrest Gump, he asked, in his characteristic charming way, "Is there a German Gump, a French Gump? Or a Japanese Gump?"

His question made me realize there are Forrest Gumps in every nation and in every heart. I have seen the film at least ten times. When it's re-run on TV, I am *compelled* to see it again. Many people feel the same way about experiencing its emotional highs and lows.

This character-driven film resonates at the deepest level. There is a happy fool in all of us. What we see in Forrest Gump is what is buried in our hidden self. There is a universal message in the movie, and, to me, it also provides therapeutic messages that make an impression on our soul and unconscious mind. The character of Forrest Gump helps us to realize a few of our special qualities in life, providing a way to view our selves and enable us not to feel insulted or lose face. This phenomenon occurs when the ego is tamed. That is, the ego is transformed from a culturally trained infant and becomes spiritualized.

Forrest Gump teaches us that a challenge in life is an opportunity to become a better person. It's another of life's tests. If we fail, no problem. The challenge will be repeated until we get it right. In the words of William Blake: "A fool persists in his folly until he becomes wise."

A mistake is an opportunity to learn a lesson. In the Thai language, there is this provocative phrase: *Phit phen khru* ('A mistake is my teacher').

Forrest Gump encourages people to be shining stars that glow from within. The opposite is being 'dimly lit.' Forrest knew how to do away with limitations and boundaries; how to fall in love with someone who could not fall in love with him; how to be successful at whatever he set his sights on.

One of my favorite books on "reel therapy" is by Gary Solomon (AKA the "Movie Doctor"). His work, *The Motion Picture Prescription: Watch This Movie And Call Me In The Morning*, is about healing messages contained in character-driven films. The following are his thoughts on *Forrest Gump*:

> *Forrest challenges us with his own challenges. We can all be a little embarrassed for the prejudice and attitude of the people around Forrest.*

Why must people be so cruel to those who are different? Forrest teaches us not to stuff our feelings inside us and not to give credit to those who would do anything to hurt us. Notice how he sees the good in people and that he always wants to be the best that he can be. That's the lesson Forrest learned and those are lessons he can teach us.

More than anything, this movie teaches us it's the little things in life that are important. Forrest also teaches us about giving, kindness, and love; love of family and love of others.

It seems to me, Forrest Gump doesn't have an unkind bone in his body. What a tremendous thing to aspire to: not being judgmental of others. How is it that someone so challenged in life could be such an inspiration? This is a special movie, one that I would like all of you to watch more than once. You cannot help but grow from the experience. I once watched the movie with my brother, Gary, who is mentally retarded. He was mesmerized.

As we know, the fictional Forrest Gump came from the womb, wounded. He was dealt a poor hand—an IQ of 75 placed him in the defective range of intelligence. While he was intellectually challenged, he became spiritually endowed as a result of his mother's training.

The non-fictional Thai equivalent of Forrest Gump, Atip Muangsuwan, was dealt a good hand at birth—certainly not in the defective range of intelligence. As I got to know this real-life Forrest Gump, I became aware of the personal qualities that make him similar in many ways to Hollywood's fictional hero.

The story began on the dance floor of La Rueda, the Mother of Latin dance clubs in Bangkok. Motanee, a lovely woman and wonderful Latin dancer said to me one night as we danced to vibrant salsa music, "Richard, if you ever have a people-problem, go to Atip."

"Who is Atip?" I asked.

"Over there. He's always smiling. He's dancing with Wasana." (Wasana is a professional Latin dancer and teacher who hangs out at La Rueda.)

After my dance, I went to the bar and observed Atip dancing. The *farang* and Thai women glowed as he swirled them around. I watched when he stepped off the dance floor and engaged in conversation with men and women in this non-pick-up club that attracts an international clientele. Two qualities about him reminded me of Forrest Gump: both had a perpetual smile and a bland look. That look is sometimes interpreted as being slow-witted. The euphemism is 'mentally challenged.' If I saw Atip on the street, I would have thought he was a simpleton. On the other hand, his look could indicate a person who sees too much. A *seer*.

I decided to check out Motanee's advice with some questions that would prove if Atip might be the Forrest Gump of Thailand. After introducing myself, I asked if he had ever seen the Oscar-winning film.

"Many times. It's my all-time favorite movie," he replied, smiling.

Since he was familiar with the film, I decided to give him my version of a personality test. "What's your interpretation of Forrest Gump's signature statement—"

Before I could complete the question, he said, "You're referring to 'Stupid is as stupid does.' Is that right?" No hesitancy. He took a swig of orange juice. "Which interpretation—the short or long one?"

"Let's start with the short one," I said.

"It means that a person has a fondness for stupidity," Atip said, beaming.

Noticing my incredulity, his smile broadened.

At that moment, Motanee came over to us with Wasana, who coaxed Atip to cha-cha with her to Santana's "Smooth."

"What do you think of Atip?" Motanee asked.

I watched Wasana put some complex moves on Atip, his Cheshire-cat smile dominating the atmosphere. "So far I'm impressed."

"Remember, go to him if you have a people-problem," she reminded me.

That was the second time she'd brought that up. I wondered if she had the psychic power of clairvoyance.

"I suppose that means that others go to him if they have a—"

"People-problem," she intoned.

After the cha-cha, I invited Atip to join me at the bar. Peter from Australia engaged Motanee in a merengue.

"Ahhh, Richard," Atip said. "Do you want to hear my long interpretation of Forrest Gump's signature statement?"

"A toast," I said, as I clinked my Singha beer bottle against his glass of orange juice.

"My meaning is that Forrest's mind—both conscious and unconscious—is zeroed in on what Buddhists call 'right mindfulness' and 'right concentration.' That is, Forrest has phenomenal control of his thoughts. When he hears a negative verbal assault made against him, he immediately clears his mind and dismisses the comment. By not giving it energy, he maintains calm in what could have turned out to be a stormy sea."

"If the person or persons were not dimly lit, the remark would not have been uttered," I said.

"By having 'right mindfulness,'" Atip continued, "which was instilled in him by his amazing mother, Forrest is never offended by verbal assaults. He has *transcended* negativity. By dismissing unhealthy, unworthy, unkind, and hostile thoughts—which are all 'wrong concentration'—he is practicing 'right concentration.'"

"Allow me to piggyback on that thought," I said.

Atip nodded.

"Forrest Gump," I said, "has a smart weapon in his behavioral arsenal. He sends a missile to disintegrate an incoming hostile weapon—in this case, a verbal assault. I guess you could say he uses a smart weapon to destroy a dumb weapon."

"Very good," Atip said.

I ordered another Singha. "Atip do you have a magical 'signature statement'?"

"As a matter of fact, I do. Do you want to hear it now or another time?"

"Now," I replied.

"I am big on the word '*un-er-stan*,'" he said. "It's the heart of conflict resolution."

According to Atip, conflict results when two people in an emotionally charged scenario misunderstand each other's point of view. Atip induces the upset twosome to listen attentively to the other's point of view. The first person must not talk, just listen. After hearing the point of view, the second person does the same.

"*Un-er-stanin'* is a two-way street," Atip said. "From *un-er-stanin'* comes wisdom."

◆

Several weeks after his explanation, the Bangkok Latin dance community was buzzing about a blow-up between a Western man and a Thai woman. The incident had taken place a few days before the November Loy Kratong festival. La Rueda was arranging a big float for the festive occasion. The salsa people's float would be launched into the Chao Phraya River, washing away the woes of all those who put their names into it alongside the incense and candles and coins for good luck. Mark ordered Noi to arrange the decoration for the float in a certain way. His request was a *demand* that was issued in a booming voice that angered her. As a result: instant disharmony.

Over the next two weeks, Noi refused to dance with Mark. She never even looked him in the eye. Resolution was impossible, as she met his attempts to patch things up with an icy glare. Then she fled from his presence.

Desperate, Mark turned to Atip, who agreed to intercede. He talked to Noi, telling her that Mark was distraught over the loss of her friendship. Mark wished for an end to the discord.

"I told her about crossing the street," Atip said, "to listen to his side of the story. Then he was to cross to her side of the street and hear her point of view."

The therapeutic session took place on the second floor of La Rueda. Salsa music filtered upstairs. Mark learned that his domineering tone and bossiness had turned off his friend and former dance partner.

"If you had spoken to me in a gentle manner, I would have done the flower arrangement your way," she said. "I would have done that because your arrangement was more imaginative than mine."

Continuing, she said, "Shouting is impolite to Thai people."

Speaking from his side of the street, Mark explained that this ordeal taught him a valuable lesson—"I need to become more Thai-like in my behavior."

"Well, Mark, how about a dance?" Noi said, taking his hand.

After relating this scenario to me, Atip asked me for my observation. I told him that, through his brand of conflict resolution, Mark was able to exorcise his demon. "Thanks to you, he will no longer get into trouble," I said. "It's possible that his character flaw of speaking harshly and trying to dominate others is gone or perhaps diminished."

I asked Atip what lesson Noi had learned from the ordeal.

"In the future," he said, "she will not hide her feelings in a confrontational situation." She would be "more *farang*" by seeking to express her emotions.

"It's not good to have hostile feelings and hold a grudge," she had told Atip.

◆

For three days, the salsa club members frolicked in the sand and surf at Koh Samet, an island resort four hours by road and ferry from Bangkok. Atip and I shared a room. After the dancing and partying ended one night, we returned to our room, and Atip's girlfriend called him to whisper endearments and bid him goodnight. She called four or five more times to tell him 'sweet dreams, my love.'

That wasn't enough. After she was finished calling, text messages came through. Atip asked if the calls and chimes announcing the arrival of SMS love notes bothered me.

I told him it was charming to see how lovesick Thai people behaved.

"Same as with lovers in the United States," he said. "In America," he continued, pounding his pillow into shape, "lovers usually kiss and have sex before marriage, right?"

"Ninety-two percent of the time, that's true."

"In America, the man inserts and the woman receives his holy projectile—yes?"

I put the lights on and looked at Atip. He was sitting at the edge of his bed. "You're telling me that you and your girlfriend have not had sex?"

"That's right."

"How long have you been dating?"

"One year already. She's a virgin; I'm a virgin. We're Thai."

"How old are you?"

"Thirty," he said, displaying his Cheshire-cat smile. "Richard, did you see the movie *Never Been Kissed*?"

"You mean to tell me that you've—"

"That's right. I've never been kissed for longer than four seconds. And never on the mouth."

He laughed and pointed to both cheeks. "In Thai society, cheek-kissing is in."

He told me about his life.

He was born and raised in Lamphun, a small town near Chiang Mai, the cultural and commercial capital of northern Thailand. "It's a small, peaceful town," he said. "I love the temples and the monks."

The American Gump was influenced by his mother, but the Thai Gump attributes his philosophical and psychological outlook to his father, who trained him in the Buddhist concepts of 'right mindfulness' and 'right concentration.' As a youth, he cycled the twenty kilometers into Chiang Mai to hang out with an American expat who helped him with English lessons. Atip attended the University of Chiang Mai, majoring in geology. He received a M.Sc. in Petroleum and Geosciences at the University of Brunei, in that oil-rich sultanate. As an earth scientist (his job title at Chevron), he uses high-tech probes and studies underwater maps to search for oil in the waters off Thailand. During his training with Chevron in Texas, Utah, and California, he made side trips to New York City, the dance Mecca in the United States, to check out the mambo and salsa scene.

A Thai virgin, I thought to myself, as I put the light out again. Just like his American counterpart.

◆

The scenario that resulted in my desperately seeking out the Forrest Gump of Thailand resulted from an article I wrote for *Metro* magazine. The story was about a close-encounter dance, the Balboa, where the partners have an intimate connection, similar to that in the tango. La Rueda's resident teacher, Alexis, is from southern California, where the Balboa originated. As a teacher, dancer, and person, Alexis is exceptional, but she was horrified when she read my interpretation of the dance that she taught with passion. When I went to class at La Rueda, after the story came out, she took me aside and read me the riot act. She said that I had made up the quotes attributed to her. "You never interviewed me," she said.

It was true; I did not interview her. Instead, during the four months of attending the class, I had taken notes. It was impossible for her to remember all of the things she said about the Balboa being a sexy, intimate dance. She also said that my mind was obviously filled with sex—which was true again, as I worship the female form. She was referring to one of my "lurid" descriptions of the Balboa: "You are close enough to the woman. Occasionally you can feel her Mound of Venus." I was proud of the exotic description. She was convinced that many men would come to the class "expecting to have sex on the dance floor." Her biggest fear was being seen as a prostitute.

Overhearing the conversation was Atip, a member of the same class. Also overhearing the dressing down were two Thai women students who loved the Balboa.

After the tongue whipping, I went to the bar. The class was to start in fifteen minutes. Alexis went to the dressing room to put on one of her outfits that the men swooned over. Motanee, also one of the Balboa participants, had the bartender play a hot number, and she invited me to warm up with her. I told her I was drowning my sorrow in suds.

"Lucky for you that Atip is here," she said, patting me on the back.

I instantly recalled her words to me several months before: "Richard, if you ever have a people problem, go to Atip."

Atip was on the floor, warming up with Wasana. He caught my glance and whispered to Wasana. The Thai Gump motioned me to follow him upstairs.

"Richard, congratulations for crossing the street to *un-er-stan'* Alexis. We all heard what was said. You un-er-stan' her position. You must ask her to cross the street so she can un-er-stan' your point of view."

Without waiting for my response, Atip went downstairs. Within a minute, Alexis was beside me, clad in a low-cut red gown, still full of fury.

I explained that I meant no harm to her. I wrote the story from my heart. I was sad and sorry that it was taken as an insult.

"You failed to mention that a donation from the lessons goes to charity," she said.

My failure to include that fact, I confessed, was due to an error of omission.

Then she surprised me by saying, "Richard, you're entitled to your interpretation of the Balboa. If someone else wrote it, there would be another interpretation."

That meant she was '*un-er-stan-in'* me.

"Alexis, I meant no harm. You see—"

A second surprise came when she hugged me, and, in a warm voice, said, "The matter's closed. Let's not discuss it anymore. Okay?"

Delighted with this outcome, I insisted on buying a bottle of Alexis's favorite white wine.

The incident taught me a valuable lesson as a writer. Since that experience, I now show my copy to any person I write about, to get feedback, before sending it to magazines.

I decided the Thai Gump is in the personal growth business.

◆

The signature method of Atip is a concept that is also practiced by Jerry Spence, the high-profile American lawyer who often appears on Larry King's show. Spence's style is to disarm an opponent by listening with *rapt attention* to what is being said. The person is usually so impressed with this approach that the same courtesy is extended in return. On the sub-conscious level, the person will thus be favorably inclined to listen to the other's point of view.

Besides being a virgin and never having been kissed on the mouth, Atip has social skills and expertise in conflict resolution without having had formal training. Like the American Gump, he lives life from the heart. He has the feminine trait of intuition.

There is another important quality the real-life Gump has in common with the fictional Gump. Both possess child-like innocence. This attribute enables them to gain access to a magical place, thus fulfilling the Buddhist and Christian prophecy that the gates of heaven will open to a person who is a child at heart. Both, metaphorically speaking, can walk on troubled waters, meaning that, in a crisis situation, they emanate serene vibes that affect others. Both are tuned to higher realities.

The American and Thai Gump lack cynicism. Other virtues are honesty and being non-judgmental. Their authenticity and genuineness wins the heart of cynical people.

I wondered what Atip's thoughts on anger were. "Thai Gump," I said, "What do you do when you become angry?"

"Ahh," he replied, "I welcome anger."

He explained that the emotion represented an opportunity for character growth. He would examine *why* he "fell" into anger. "Lord Buddha," he said, "taught that everybody is a potential Buddha."

Atip is able to find light even in darkness.

Roger Ebert, the celebrated cinema critic, made this profound statement in his review of the classic film: "I've never met anyone like Forrest Gump in a movie before."

To paraphrase Ebert, I have never met anyone in real life like Atip Muangsuwan.

Thailand's Spiritual Banker

I watched as the fly landed on Janet's tranquil face and wondered if she would swat the pest away or, at least, make twitches or grimaces that would disturb the uninvited guest.

The fly paraded along her left cheek, but Janet did not swat, nor did she grimace.

To my continued awe, nary a twitch. The fly strolled leisurely until it stopped for a brief rest on Janet's right cheek. The journey included a walk over her nose.

All the while I sat there, in disbelief.

Then, of its own volition, the fly departed and landed on another meditator's face, a young Brit on a three-month holiday in the kingdom. The Brit's meditation was interrupted as his hand made a serious swipe. Getting the message, the fly escaped untouched. The Brit resumed his meditation.

Back to Janet. There was fifteen minutes left in this session at a resort in Nakhon Nayok, a scenic area a couple of hours by road from Bangkok. I prayed for another 'bug happening.' Happily, my selfish prayer was answered in double fashion. Some kind of tropical bug appeared on her bare right leg. Another species of tropical splendor crashed into her bare right arm. Both crawled in earnest. One of the bugs took a brief flight to Janet's face, strolling down the bridge of her nose. Not a wince due to the nose bug or the creature traversing her arm.

Squirming with delight now, I prayed that the bug enter her nose and burrow inside the dark cavern. How would this Buddha-in-training react to this emergency?

Prayer not answered. What a pity.

Janet remained serene; there should have been havoc and chaos. I took a look at the other eleven group members. By their grimaces and movements, it was obvious which ones were bugged by the bugs.

Then I looked at Tony U-Thasoonthorn, the founder of the International Meditation Club, and 'Spiritual Banker' (his legally registered trademark) for both the corporate world and individuals. He grinned, indicating 'I-told-you-about-Janet.'

Corporations like Mattel and Sara Lee go to Tony. He opens a 'spiritual account' for the workers of a firm, then each worker makes deposits to enrich their spiritual, emotional, and material life. The same is true with an individual who seeks out Tony. Like with the corporate workers, Tony shows people how to open a spiritual bank account. Then the extraordinary teacher trains them how to make deposits into the account.

Before the meditation session had started, Tony took me aside and told me that Janet would not be bugged by the bugs.

I had said, "Impossible, Tony."

He suggested that I observe her.

When the exercise ended, we gathered in a circle. Tony asked who wanted to talk about the thirty-minute experience.

I told the group what I'd seen during my spy mission. Janet was never disturbed or distracted by the aerial bombardment and expeditions of flies and bugs. They had no mercy toward her, but she had mercy on them.

Tony asked if Janet wished to share how she accomplished this feat.

An attractive blonde in her late twenties, Janet worked as a computer programmer for a big-name American company based in Bangkok. Modest and unassuming, she intoned the words frequently used by the Spiritual Banker: "Attention and intention."

Tony, in his soft voice that purred into our sub-conscious (thus making us consciously aware), stressed that we have the ability to reclaim power that was lost to us when we left the Garden of Eden in our early youth. In literary and religious terms, the 'loss of innocence.'

He told us that, when entering meditation, we should silently intone, 'My intention is to keep my mind focused. When a thought enters, greet it and let is pass. A thought is likened to a guest that comes to your party. With polite and deliberate intention, you greet but do not spend time with the new arrival. That would be discourteous to the other new arrivals.'

We were told that when, eventually, no more guests arrive, the mind will focus on emptiness or 'nothingness.' Our 'intention' will lead to the slowing down of inner speech and we will find the place where serenity dwells. I thought about the meditation ideal of expanding the empty space between thoughts.

Tony asked Janet, "What did you say to yourself when the bugs crawled on your face and your body?"

Janet said, "My intention was to let the bugs disappear when they wanted to. I refused to pay attention to them."

"Hmmm," I said aloud. "I wonder if that mind trickery will work for me."

"Or me," a man from Sweden said.

"In your next meditative session," Tony said, "perhaps all of you can invoke the sacred words. . . ."

We all chanted at the same time: "Attention and intention."

◆

The next morning, we gathered at a waterfall in the mountains for another meditation exercise. The setting reminded me of the idyllic waterfalls on the Hawaiian isle of Kauai.

Sure enough, a bug banged into my cheek (left one). Forewarned, I mentally talked to myself—'My intention is to let the bug not bug me. It will disappear when it's ready to move on.'

Sorry to report that the invocation did not help. The bug bugged me. Then another thought came from somewhere: 'Your intention can be stated this way—the bug is an angel. Angels tread lightly.'

What a far-out insight. It's what Tony calls "insight meditation."

'My intention,' I repeated, 'is that the bug is—'

Before I could finish the divine thought, I felt nothing on my cheek. A few minutes later, another uninvited guest paraded onto my right arm. 'My intention is that the visitor is an angel that treads lightly.' Sure enough, the bug crawling on me amounted to an angel floating on my arm. I knew, as knowing knows, that the bug was still on my body. I also knew that its angelic touch was too light for me to feel.

A common meditative miracle.

During the after-meditation round-up, it was learned that all of us became like Janet.

The power of the *trained* mind at work. The power of energy at work. The power that came from being with Tony.

◆

Tony suggested that I interview Kate, a diplomat from a Western country. Kate told me that two days after the 2004 tsunami wrecked parts of southern Thailand, she was sent to help the citizens of her country who were caught up in the disaster. In her mid-twenties, Kate was a rising star in her post. One of the two medical doctors in the embassy was also assigned to the job.

The tsunami assignment was supposed to be for one month. After two weeks, she had to be recalled to the embassy in Bangkok. What she had seen and experienced down south had made her a "virtual basket case." When bodies washed ashore on the beaches of Phuket, they were bloated and horribly disfigured. The equatorial sun had caused many defilements. Fish had feasted on parts of the corpses.

The stench was unbearable, as was the nauseating sight of the physical destruction. It was impossible to identify any of the corpses—except for a friend of Kate's who, regrettably, had taken a holiday from the embassy the day before the tsunami struck. The friend was identified from her bracelet with dolphins. The images haunted Janet day and night. All this, combined with horror stories from the survivors, contributed to her emotional and mental deterioration.

The doctor also suffered from trauma. He and Kate were offered counseling from the embassy's staff psychiatrist. The traumatized doctor responded quickly. Kate's condition worsened. She was put on medical leave. The psychiatrist recommended that Kate return home for hospitalization. He gave two diagnoses: morbid PTSS (post-traumatic stress syndrome) and severe depression that might take the form of a vegetative state.

"I didn't want to go home as a basket case," she told me.

A friend gave her a brochure about Tony's three-day meditation retreat at Jomtien Beach, next to Pattaya.

"When I left on the bus, a song that I had forgotten about kept repeating itself," Kate said. "It was my mother's favorite tune—"I Believe In Miracles.""

During her first attempt at 'walking meditation' on the soft sands of Jomtien, Kate kept falling down. "What a horrible situation. Why couldn't I walk?" she told me.

During the after-meditation round-up at Jomtien, Kate had shared her problem.

"Could it be," Tony asked her, "that you are carrying the burden of the world on your back?"

Kate had been stunned by this unexpected truth.

"Then the *impossible* happened," she said. "Tony asked me to sing my favorite song."

She hadn't mentioned her mother's favorite song to him or anyone else.

After singing "I Believe In Miracles," she received a rousing ovation.

"Each sound was a surge of warmth within me."

Tony told her that meditation helps in lifting the burdens one carries. Kate's stumbling and falling was due to the heavy suitcases—called thoughts and emotions—that she was carrying. In meditation, by letting go of crippling baggage, the mind becomes free. The heavy weights are discarded. You tell yourself that your 'intention' is to let go of the past.

The intention, even for a beginner in meditation, is to increase 'right mindfulness' through a willingness to give things away. As the excess baggage is discarded, the mind begins to feel lighter. The body is also lighter.

This technique lays the foundation for the mind to become serene and placid. Tony refers to this as building the first floor of a multi-level house. The goal of sustained attention on the present moment enables the mind to slow down. Eventually, one aims to produce the fruit of "having no history." No past and no future. Only the present moment.

Having opened her spiritual bank account, Tony then reminded Kate and the others that it was their responsibility to make deposits on a regular basis. Twenty minutes a day would lighten the mind from ceaseless inner chatter. Twenty minutes a day to slow down the mind. Such is the promise.

Within a week of leaving the beach scene, Kate was taken off various medications and back on the job. *Don't you believe in miracles? I do.* The psychiatrist withdrew his request to have her sent home for hospitalization. Truly, meditation is medication.

During a follow-up coffee chat, Kate told me that "having no history" of the past during meditation was worth a try. Every time she entered the meditative state, she declared—'my intention is to focus on the present moment.'

◆

Fritz, in his mid-forties, had the same problem as Kate with the walking meditation on the sands of Jomtien Beach. Like Kate, he had stumbled and fallen repeatedly. Unlike Kate, his problem was due to chronic alcoholism for the previous fifteen years.

Before proceeding, 'walking meditation' needs to be defined. The meditator walks in slow motion for one hundred yards. Upon reaching a marked spot, he pauses, then returns to the beginning. The process is repeated for thirty minutes.

At the start of walking meditation, the meditator lowers his eyes to a spot a few feet ahead. Before taking the first step, this is said: 'My intention is to move my right foot slowly forward. When my foot touches the ground, I slowly move my left foot forward, and it too, is off the ground.' Each foot hovers in mid-air momentarily. Upon reaching the designated spot, 100 yards away, the person stops and intones, 'My intention is to turn. I turn the right foot halfway round. I turn the foot again until I face the opposite direction.'

When pointed in the return direction, the command of intention is invoked again: 'My intention is to walk slowly and deliberately.'

Walking meditation requires balance and co-ordination, as each foot is suspended in the air before landing.

"The walking meditation made me see my life in slow motion," Fritz said. "I kept stumbling and falling."

The cause of his loss of balance and poor co-ordination, he confessed, was due to heavy intake of alcohol.

"For the first time in fifteen years," he said, "I realized that I was living in a state of total denial."

He asked Tony what he should do.

"When you get back to your room," Tony said, "perform a thirty-minute lying down meditation. Tomorrow morning, you and the group will have another walking meditation. You will see the difference in your performance."

The next day, Fritz did see a difference. He completed the thirty-minute walking meditation totally upright.

◆

I was also present during the remarkable transformation of James from Australia. His Thai wife, Sanya, and his two-year-old son accompanied him on the trip. Mother and son did not participate in the meditations. They were the beneficiaries of his change from an ill-tempered and impatient man who tended to fly into a rage.

By seeing his life in slow motion during three sessions of walking meditation at Nakhon Nayok, he experienced his life "in review." He related to the movie *Groundhog Day*, starring Bill Murray. In this film, Murray is disliked by his co-workers, especially women, for many reasons. He is selfish, egotistical, shows contempt for others, and is insulting. These are his major character flaws.

"Above all," James the Aussie said, "the character in the movie was ill-tempered, mean-spirited, and insensitive to others."

James said that he could never see how his flaws affected his wife, son, and others in his life. Through the movie, the faults of Bill Murray—and his own—were obvious.

"That's the advantage of seeing a movie that has healing messages," Tony said. "You can see yourself through the person in the story."

Meditation is medication.

At the same session, Ana from Hana (Maui, Hawaii) told her story.

Ana reported that she was an expert at disguising her personality flaws. She admitted to petty jealousies, bad-mouthing others behind their backs, and wishing ill will to those she disliked. "And," she said, twirling a lock of golden hair, "I curse my misfortune in being beautiful. I always think that guys are after me for only one reason."

"She's been showing the group her 'persona'—the mask she wears," Tony said.

Ana tousled her hair. "And I can be a real bitch with a capital 'B.' Shall I go on and bring out more of my dirty linen?"

"You're telling us," I said, "about the beast behind the beauty."

"Exactly," she said. "My dark side overtakes me at times. A Jekyll and Hyde I am."

When she had returned to Bangkok from her first retreat, Ana was seized with the desire to do all the three meditations—walking, sitting, and (Tony's favorite) lying in bed.

"Ana's right," Tony said. "In the reclining position, I don't even have to get out of bed to meditate. Sorry, Ana, please continue."

"I would meditate from twenty to forty minutes," Ana went on. "After a week of walking, sitting, and in-bed meditations, I began to feel a strange 'lightness of being.' I felt so light that I imagined I was floating."

She turned to Tony, her body language and expression indicating she wished him to tell what was taking place in her consciousness.

Tony told us that Ana had reached the stage where "defilements" and impurities were making a hasty exit from her mind.

"All of us have what Buddhism calls defilements and impurities," Tony explained. "In Western terms, they are known as character defects. Remember what James told us about the character in *Groundhog Day*. That person's flaws—or defilements and impurities—consisted of selfishness, egocentricity, a haughty disdain for others, and mocking people. As the movie progressed, we saw the character's flaws being diminished until they were extinguished."

James interjected: "Ana doesn't have any of those deplorable impurities and defilements."

Ana giggled.

Fritz added, "Ana is pure in heart and mind."

More giggles from Ana. "But I *do* have defilements and impurities, even though they are hidden."

Some gasps were heard, especially from me.

"Ana," Tony said, "was feeling lighter because these defilements were disappearing from her mind and consciousness. She is now reaching the stage in meditation known as 'beauty.'"

All in the group wanted Tony to elaborate on reaching beauty in meditation.

We were told that our inner essence of beauty, joy, and ecstasy is reached when the mind is still and empty of thoughts. The mind "fills" us with these fruits of the spirit during those moments of stillness.

This stage is better known as the "full sustained intention on the beautiful moment."

According to Tony, a moment of beauty can manifest itself as a white light, a blue pearl, or a similar vision of intense pleasure. We are put into a state of rapture or bliss.

"Don't worry if this experience doesn't occur in your second week of meditation, or second month, or second year, or second decade. Keep on keeping on."

Tony added these words to his mantra: "Meditation is medication for the mind."

Tony then pointed out a couple of known facts: the speed of sound (in air) is 700 miles per hour. Light (in a vacuum) travels at a speed of 186,282 miles per second. But a different, abstract fact is that the mind 'travels' or reacts at a speed that approaches infinity. He gave the example of looking at the stars on a clear night. We see, through the mind, hundreds of stars. Some of them have taken thousands of light years to become visible from our planet. If we turn our head a mere two inches, our mind will perceive hundreds of more stars. While we perceive this, we also feel the sensation of a breeze striking our face; we hear water cascading down the waterfall; or sounds of people talking. Our mind can also imagine the taste of a pizza that is being cooked nearby. In that same instant, our mind can entertain yet another thought or image.

◆

Tony U-Thasoonthorn is his full name. I thought it was a mix of Burmese and Thai, but Tony told me, "It's a totally Thai name given to my grandfather by King Rama VI. The meaning is 'The Eloquent Speaker—Utha Soonthorn.'"

This 'Eloquent Speaker' is attracted to both capitalism and spirituality. Materialism and the workings of the spirit, he believes, should co-exist. Instead of one being profane and the other sacred, Tony sees business and commerce as sacred as spirituality. Back in the 1980s, to prove his point, he and his then-wife operated a Montessori school that had an enrollment of 300 pupils. Tony also worked in the corporate world as a banker.

His gurus and mentors in meditation included a Thai Buddhist 'forest monk,' a Tibetan lama in the United States, and a Hindu ascetic in the Himalayas. A true 'eclectic.'

When he returned to Thailand in 2001, without his American wife, the urge to get others involved in meditation was realized. He founded the International Meditation Club and started weekend retreats at first-class hotels and resorts in scenic spots throughout Thailand.

Mattel, the maker of the Barbie doll and other toys sold worldwide, sent twenty of its Thai, American, and European staff for meditation training. The two-day workshop took place at the posh beach resort at Jomtien. According to an article in the *International Herald Tribune*, Tony was chosen over psychiatrists and other top motivational consultants because of his reputation for making a positive impact in reducing stress and releasing creative energy. Arunagiri Manikam, Mattel's general manager in Thailand, wanted to make his employees clear-minded, relaxed, creative, and easier to get along with. These goals could be achieved by having Tony reduce the staff's stress levels.

Arunagiri could have hired a team of psychiatrists to visit his employees, but instead he decided to experiment with meditation training. Giving his employees a free weekend meditation course provided opportunities for self-exploration, which is essential to running a productive business. "It's important to recharge the batteries," he said.

In the 'audition' interview with Mattel, Tony told his client: "There are noises we don't like, annoying people in other departments, the air-con that is too cold. If you don't let go of all that is negative, it gnaws at you and you can't concentrate on your work. Meditation can release the worker from all that mental pollution.

"Meditation can only lead to good things. Not only will it help employees work better, but it will strengthen their minds. They will spread peace to one another in the workplace, then to the society, and eventually to the world."

First-time meditator, Jantima Kaewpradad, signed up for the Mattel company's second workshop "out of desperation." She saw the first group return to the factory calmer than when they had left, and wanted to know the secret.

"How can you concentrate on one thing?" she said. "My life is very messy: two managers left, and I have to handle too many things.

I am attending an MBA workshop, and have three kids. I cannot manage my time."

"Normally I'm cool," said a warehouse worker, "but maybe after this, I will be very cool."

Farah Bakar attended the first Mattel retreat and believed her life had changed for the better. Now she meditates fifteen minutes a day and as needed in the office—such as when she senses herself growing frustrated with people who fire off "thoughtless" questions, or when she is annoyed by the constantly ringing phone. "Previously I got moody all the time; I would shout at everyone. Now I feel like I can calm down. People call me because they need me, not because they mean to bother me. I've changed my style."

Another woman divulged that she felt nothing at all and couldn't get her mind to quiet down.

"There is no right or wrong way to meditate," assured Tony. "You can't change the world, but you can change yourself and the world will look different."

Arunagiri, convinced of the effectiveness of the two workshops, said he would be sending another 240 staffers to the meditation express.

◆

Most teachers, tapes, and books on meditation expound the technique of 'watching your breath'—meaning that you focus your attention on the nostrils and pay attention to the rising and falling of the breath. Another option is to observe the rising and falling of the abdomen. A third option is to visualize a balloon in front of your chest; visualize it expanding and contracting as you breathe in and out.

A fourth method is to imagine *no object* in front of your chest. "An object will appear within a short time," Tony claimed. "You can focus your attention on what your mind conjures up."

When we tire of 'watching' and 'observing' the breath or balloon, we can go into "loving-kindness" meditation. Tony sees this as an art form. That's one of the reasons he has phenomenal success. The loving-kindness art form produces insights galore. By practicing loving kindness, negative thoughts, including ill feelings toward others (and our selves) are transformed—making us kinder, gentler, and more loving.

Upon returning home to my Bangkok apartment, I discovered, to my amazement, that meditation had become easy. I began doing it twice a day for thirty minutes each session. Before taking a nap, I would do in-bed meditation for twenty minutes, thus making three daily deposits in my spiritual account. I agreed with the Eloquent Speaker that watching the breath, or the abdomen rising and falling, could be boring. What worked for me was loving kindness.

Like Tony told us, time doesn't matter. In meditation there is no past, no future. There is only the present moment of sustained attention. This comes about through the magical incantation— 'intention.'

Another aspect of insight meditation is that the mind bestows its gifts upon us. As a writer, ideas constantly bubble up. For a composer, musical 'happenings' will float to consciousness; for business people, important revelations surface from the sub-conscious. Creative ideas will bubble up for all of us. That's one of the reasons the GM of Mattel decided to engage Tony's services.

Happy to report that I have become a meditation addict. I meditate from seven minutes to seventy minutes a day. Like Tony, my favorite form is in-bed meditation.

◆

One night, when Tony and several of us student meditators were having dinner at a social event in Bangkok, he received a call on his mobile phone. From his expression, I sensed that this was a spiritual crisis from one of his other students. The 'Banker' excused himself and went outside. I followed him on a spy mission to eavesdrop on the conversation. Sure enough, Tony proved to be an expert in telephone therapy.

When he came back to the table, Tony explained that he had made a "spiritual loan" to the person he'd been talking to—an art form that is achieved by practicing random acts of kindness and performing senseless acts of beauty. A ripple effect is achieved by being gentle and displaying warmth in our daily encounters. By enriching others, we enrich ourselves.

Ways of making a spiritual loan can include a simple smile or giving up a seat on a bus or train. Or offering advice or just an empathic ear. My favorite way of making a spiritual loan is to 'stop my mouth,' meaning that I will not speak or act in anger. There is a Zen saying: "A closed mouth fails to attract a fist or a foot."

The recipient of a spiritual loan pays back by giving of himself to another person, who, in turn, makes a spiritual loan to a third party. Thus, all of us become 'Spiritual Ambassadors Extraordinaire.'

The mind has awesome 'Power.' Through meditation and the simple technique of loving kindness, as taught by the Spiritual

Banker, the mind can be slowed down from its usual chaotic state of inner dialogue, ridding us of intrusive and unwanted thoughts and emotions. The excessive baggage that all of us are burdened with is lightened. This 'miracle' is accomplished by making regular deposits in our spiritual bank account. By doing this, our inner beauty is released. Heaven on earth is no longer a fantasy.

We know Tony's favorite words: 'attention' and 'intention.' And 'meditation is medication.'

The Eloquent Speaker has spoken.

The Sex Baron And
The Beauty-Shop Owner

THE PRE-DAWN SNEAK attack on the fateful Sunday of January 26, 2003 caused the world of Panich Khunshi, 44, to come tumbling down. In a well-orchestrated, commando-style raid, rogue members of the Thai police and army, along with a demolition team manning bulldozers and other earth-moving equipment, stormed into Bangkok's "Sukhumvit Square," a city block of beer bars and other small businesses located between Soi 8 and 10 on one of the city's main thoroughfares.

By daylight, the destruction was complete. Hundreds of shops (and all their contents and stock) had been reduced to a flat layer of rubble in just two hours. Included in the debris were beer bars, beauty salons, Internet cafés, dry cleaners and laundry stores, restaurants, jewelry stores, and antique and souvenir shops. City commuters and passers-by were shocked at the scene. The media showed the faces of disbelieving owners and employees reporting to Sukhumvit Square for what they thought would be just another routine 'day at the office.'

Captured in newspaper photos and freeze-framed television shots was the anguished face of Panich Khunshi, the owner of a beauty salon and foot-massage parlor. A mere eight months before, Panich had invested her life savings of 400,000 baht into the business. Thirty inlaid bamboo tiles valued at 200 US dollars each were turned into powder. The designer chairs were twisted and gnarled. Nothing at all was salvageable; the wreckers had struck with the force of a whirling tornado and a man-made tsunami combined.

"I thought working for myself was the answer," Panich said in a newspaper report. She had toiled for fifteen years, perfecting her skills as a hair stylist, in the employ of others.

Also put out of work were hundreds of beer bar hostesses, and staff in the varied other establishments on the site.

Panich, instead of panicking, called her 24-year-old son, a monk of four years, at his upcountry temple in Korat, northeastern Thailand. "I thought I'd committed a terrible sin and was being punished," she confessed to her son.

Her son told her the story about the Buddhist man whose house burned to the ground. Instead of lamenting his misfortune, the man, in true Buddhist fashion, stood in the midst of the ruins. Looking skyward, he said, 'I can see the heavens from my new vantage point.'

"The man used tragedy to elevate his soul. Mother, do you understand the deeper meaning?"

"No, son."

'Deepeer meaning' came a day later. In a flash of internal lightning, Panich marshaled her energy and administrative ingenuity. She managed to obtain an immediate settlement from the mastermind of the blitz.

"It was only 170,000 baht that I received. But that was enough to open my new beer bar."

◆

The man who orchestrated the pre-dawn raid at Sukhumvit Square is Chuwit Kamsolvisit, the owner of the site. He wanted the land back from the numerous vendors who had set up shop there. He has been described as an Asian Burt Reynolds; he is compared to Donald Trump. He is seen by some as a ruthless businessman, but as a Robin Hood to many of his staff and hundreds of women who served in his entertainment venues in various capacities. To some, Chuwit represented the worst feature of the kingdom by being one of the major players in the sex industry.

When he studied for his MBA at San Diego State University, the savvy Chuwit learned how franchises were set up. He picked the brains of visiting entrepreneurs, and did the same with the faculty; he networked with fellow students. He never tired of cultivating friendships. When he returned to Thailand, he opened his first lavish massage parlor. Then another and another. They were given glitzy names like "Victoria's Secret" and "Copacabana." The buildings were massive and multi-leveled. They were 'entertainment palaces.'

Every customer received the red-carpet treatment. The lounges were a delight. A client could have a drink, then select one of the girls dressed in seductive attire behind the glass windows (the 'fish bowls').

Chuwit bribed the police and politicos with money, drinks, and gifts, including the favors of his massage girls, who took extra special care of the VIP guests.

In the aftermath of the Soi 10 destruction—and as a result of the criticism he received from the authorities and the press—Chuwit took up politics, to fight back at those critics he saw as hypocrites. Many were customers at his establishments. He had incurred the wrath of the powers that be, but instead of cowering to them, Chuwit became openly defiant—by exposing them as corrupt officials who were on the take. He became the darling of the press when he announced that he would name some of the most corrupt ones. In one not-so-subtle teaser, he gave the media the first-name initial of one high-profile customer: "A high-ranking police official in the district of [he named the district] with the initial of 'B' has been on my payroll for the last year," he said.

All the officials in that district with the initial 'B' for their first name were terrified.

The press didn't have too much trouble speculating on who the mystery man was.

In one interview, when asked if sex was occurring in his massive entertainment venues, he quipped, "A man and a woman are in a room together. It's not possible for me to inspect every room to see if misbehavior of any kind is happening."

"In that case, sir," the interviewer said, "why don't you have your staff investigate the matter."

"My staff assures me every day that their inspections have not revealed any misbehavior. I trust my staff."

The media and public howled at such bravado.

Chuwit then tackled the army and elected officials. The public delighted in his theatrics. He soon became a television personality. In one strange incident, he claimed that he had been kidnapped from his car, drugged, and left abandoned on an upcountry highway. He was found wandering by the roadside. He was adamant that this was a warning from certain powerful people who remained nameless.

When he ran for the top prize, to be the governor of Bangkok, Chuwit sold all of his entertainment establishments. One journalist put it to him that "a crooked man shouldn't be in a responsible position of trust." Chuwit fired back: "That's why I should be elected. It takes a crook to catch a crook."

"What will you do with all of your entertainment places?"

"As you know, I've sold them. And I've told the new owners exactly how bribing officialdom is done. I also told them other dark secrets of the trade."

In one of his campaign posters, Chuwit was seen smashing a bathtub to pieces with a sledgehammer—a striking visual metaphor that signaled to the public he was cleaning up his act and getting out of the massage business.

He astounded the pundits by coming third in the gubernatorial vote, with thirty percent of the vote. He is now seen as a political threat in Bangkok.

Chuwit Kamsolvisit made amends at the demolition site on Sukhumvit Square. Instead of erecting another luxury hotel or office block or condominium tower—just like everywhere else on Sukhumvit Road—he built a public park that delights the eyes.

He has become a permanent player in the highly dubious game of Thai politics, and he continues to be the talk of the town.

◆

Panich's new beer bar—or 'bar beer' as the Thais say—is located in the gloomy netherworld under the expressway near the railway line that intersects the beginning of Sukhumvit Road. This surreal strip of low-rent beer bars is known locally as 'Soi Zero.' In Panich's Friends Bar, a pool table takes up most of the space. She employs four or five hostesses, and opens at four each afternoon. Despite the roaring traffic above the string of beer bars, no sound penetrates through to this 'underground cavern.'

Panich thought that she must have sinned terribly to have been the recipient of such woeful luck. Sitting at the bar, she told me in her low voice: "But my girls not commit sin."

In her customary manner of understatement, she pointed out that many men from the USA, UK, Australia, New Zealand, and a host of European and other countries flock to the Land of Smiles because they have lost hope of putting their arms around a woman in their homeland. Look, stare, gawk, dream, and fantasize about women. This is the way it is in the 'Lands of Frowns.'

Panich sees herself as a healer, making merit by performing a valuable service to men in dire need. "Many *farang* say to me, 'Panich, my dream of being with a woman comes true in Thailand.'"

After some prying, it was learned that the hostesses can make up to 30,000 baht a month. As reported in *The Nation* on December 28, 2003, Panich's daily take from her bar is a mere 700 baht. Compare this to the amount that made its way to her coffers in her beauty parlor, where she could make in excess of 3,000 baht per day.

"My money comes from the 400-baht bar fine," she said, "and beer sales, forty baht from each 'lady drink,' and twenty baht for each pool game."

I asked if she hired herself out, making herself available like the other bargirls.

"Cannot," she said. "Never, never."

"Why not?"

"I never sleep with *farangs* or Thais. Not my job."

"How about once in a while? What about going to bed for fun?" I asked.

"Cannot. Only sleep with man I love." She poured herself a coke with ice and stirred the cubes with a straw. "I look for romance."

In a sad tone she continued: "Big problem. *Farang* men not like me. Thai men not like me." Panich pointed to two girls, midriffs exposed, shooting pool. Classic Thai—slim waists, svelte, sexy, raven-haired, and young.

After exploring the subject, it was learned that Panich's concern is to make sure that her girls are taken care of. It was not proper for the owner to take business away from her workers.

Panich hopes to save enough to open another beauty shop, but the remote location under the expressway and the paucity of foot traffic combines to conspire against her realizing her wish. (During the five times Friends was visited for this story, there were never more than two customers. On three of those five visits, the place was deserted.)

The discussion got around to HIV. Panich has a strict policy. All the girls report to a clinic weekly for testing. If tested positive, the pink slip is given.

"What if a customer refuses to wear a condom?" I asked

Panich requires that the girl phone her. "I tell the customer, 'You have one life to live. The girl has one life to live. Not use condom is to lose freedom. You not want that, right? Have the lady put condom on you. I hang up now.'"

I asked Panich how she succeeded in getting the man responsible for the demolition to compensate her with 170,000 baht. She had accomplished a feat that no others equaled.

"Not difficult," she said. "I go Chuwit's office every day. He not want to look at me. I not pretty sight."

She poured herself another coke. I ordered another beer. Within seconds, a luscious lass served me a bottle of Chang, one of the local brews.

"I made myself more ugly," Panich said, "and put on ugly clothes. Chuwit not want to go office to see ugly woman wait for him. People in the office not like to see me also. All unhappy."

"It was a shake-down," I said, extending my glass to her. "*Chai yo*, Panich."

Glasses clinked.

She sipped her coke with a puzzled expression. "What's it mean, 'shake-down'?"

I explained that she had tightened the screws; instead of using strong-armed tactics favored by the mob, she played it cool by using psychological strategy.

"You out-witted Chuwit, Panich. Clever. *Geng maak.*"

She was tickled.

"You demolished the demolition man."

She liked that, too.

My Thai Girlfriend

THREE MONTHS after going out with Lek, I met her sister, brother-in-law, and their three children. Their names were in tune with the Thai tradition of having fun nicknames—sister, Gong; son, M; another son, Gun; the daughter, Pear. The brother-in-law's nickname is Mikey.

Mikey, who is in the import-export business, drew me aside and said, "Richard, you are lucky to have a Thai girlfriend."

His candid comment dumbfounded me, rendering me unable to make an intelligible response. I tried to formulate something coherent, but could not. Mikey's comment was provocative and, above all, intriguing.

Lek and I get together at my place every Wednesday evening. She stays over Wednesday and Thursday, and leaves on Friday morning.

One Wednesday, she pranced in and showed me a heavy tome she was carrying. "I learn English," she said.

After discarding her blouse and skirt, she showed me the two-pound textbook. While I browsed it, she opened a notebook and asked, "Opposite heavy?"

"Light."

"Opposite fat?"

"Skinny or thin."

"Spell, please."

This went on for a half-hour. That night we watched Al Pacino in *Scent Of A Woman*. In the film, Pacino used the military term 'H.U.A.' He explained the meaning: "'H' means I heard you. 'U' means I understand you. 'A' means I acknowledge you." After the movie, Lek got out her notebook and pounded out words for opposite meanings. Words like "stew-bid."

"Honey, there's no word 'stew-bid.'"

She referred to her Thai-English dictionary and showed me the English word 'stupid.'

"Honey, the opposite of 'stew-bid' is 'smart.'"

She tried to spell 'smart.' It came out 'sock.'

"A sock," I said, pointing to my bare feet "is what you wear over your foot."

"My English very bad," she said, discouraged. Then her eyes brightened. "Your Thai very bad."

That was true. Many times when I spoke Thai, she wanted to know if I was speaking English. The reverse was true. Quite often I thought she was speaking Thai, but it was English.

Then she'd say, "I teach honey Thai."

And I'd say, "I'm teaching honey English."

"Both very bad teachers."

◆

Christmas was approaching in the year 2004—which is 2547 in the Buddhist calendar. I received a cryptic phone call from my good friend, Joker John Hudson. He asked if I had read the e-mail he'd sent two hours before.

I had not opened my e-mail. "Joker, is it about your birthday party?" I asked.

"Full details are in the e-mail. Suzy and I have two Thai babes dying to meet you. Bye."

I was intrigued by the details he spelled out in the e-mail:

> *At my birthday and Christmas party, you can dance with two attractive women. Both are named Lek. One Lek speaks better English than the other Lek. I wonder which one you'll choose. That is, if you decide that you want a steady girlfriend. Suzy and I agree which one you'll prefer. Both are expert foot massage workers. They rent a space run by a katoey who owns a beauty salon down the road from our pad. Denis is coming with his new girlfriend.*

Which pair of dancing shoes should I take? The black and white? Or the gold and black? I decided to take both pairs.

◆

I cannot see a fly in flight, even if it's one of those big ugly ones. The only person I know who has this phenomenal visual ability is

Joker John. Truth is, at the party in two days, anyone who didn't know this would be enthralled. Joker John not only sees a fly flying, he can *swat it dead while it is airborne.* For additional entertainment, he can spot where the fly lands on the wall. How do I know this? Joker has demonstrated it time and time again. If a fly ever pestered me or anyone else, Joker blew his imaginary trumpet, sounding the cavalry charge. The bothersome flies that pestered us would be targeted and shown no mercy. It's always fun to be around Joker and Suzy.

I hoped and prayed that an unsuspecting fly would drop in at his party. He would first tell what he could do—and then show us.

◆

When I arrived at the party in the late afternoon, Joker was in a state of rapture from having a foot massage by one Lek. Suzy was also in a heavenly state from being massaged by the other Lek.

Both Leks greeted me in Thai fashion; I returned the *wais.*

I put my Christmas presents under the miniature tree. Following our usual custom, we had not spent more than 300 baht on each other's gifts.

Lek who was massaging Joker John was more petite than Lek working on Suzy. Lek working on Suzy was 'un-Thai' in that she had ample cleavage and broad hips—well endowed physically. The word lek means 'little.' So I decided to call one Lek, 'Lek Lek' (Little Lek), and her friend, 'Lek Yai' (Big Lek). Both liked the idea of being recognized by their difference.

Ying, Suzy's 21-year-old daughter, came into the living room of the spacious two-storey townhouse in the Pak Kred section of Bangkok. Under normal traffic conditions, it takes me an hour to arrive from my apartment in the Sukhumvit area. Today, under heavy traffic, it took three hours. Because of the congestion in this city of twelve million, no one is given a frown or scowl for being late. In fact, being late is not part of the Thai lexicon.

Ying brought me a glass of Cheers, my favorite Thai beer. (When I am in Cambodia, I drink Love Beer. No kidding, that's the name of the Khmer beer.)

I asked Ying (her father is Thai) to show me some of her textbooks written in English. She was a second-year engineering student at the prestigious Kasetsart University. The work was so demanding that eighty percent of her class of 100 students had dropped out or were forced to change their major due to academic woes.

Suzy asked me to try her new creation—fresh soy milk. She was about to get up from her foot massage when Ying told her mom that she would bring me a glass instead. The soy milk was surprisingly good. Suzy announced that she had made it in her nutrition class the day before. That's when I found out that she was enrolled in a degree course in nutrition at Bangkok's Sukhothai University.

"In the back yard, I grow soy beans. Organic. No pesticides in the soil."

I observed the two Leks as they massaged Joker and Suzy. Little Lek had a boyish figure, and was pixie-like. When she glanced at me, I liked the glow in her eyes. She had a girlish habit of covering her mouth with her hand when she giggled or laughed.

Big Lek was wholesome physically. She too had a winning smile. On one level she seemed to be more outgoing than Little Lek, but, and this is a paradox, she seemed to be more reserved—that is, secretive, as though she had something to hide. This was obvious when I looked into her eyes.

Excitement erupted when Denis Morris, the UK composer and bandleader, who has traveled the world many times, arrived with Ladda, his new girlfriend.

Ladda's body was as boyish as Little Lek's. She wore a sweater and a scarf over her blouse. I noticed that she focused on Big Lek's breasts. Then she gazed with adoring eyes at the ample cleavage of Suzy. When Ying came to offer the new arrivals refreshment, Ladda was spellbound by the student's cleavage, too. Indeed, Ying's breasts were balloons, dwarfing her mother and Big Lek.

Denis explained that Ladda was scheduled to have her breasts enlarged in a few days. By New Year 2005, her dream of cleavage would be realized. Now it made sense why Ladda eyed the other women and covered herself with the blouse, sweater, and scarf.

To Joker's dismay, the massaging stopped when Ladda withdrew a brochure from her purse and gave it to Suzy.

"Oh, my God," Suzy said. "It's got pictures of breasts to choose from."

"Including different sized nipples," Denis said.

At Suzy's suggestion, all the women gathered on the front terrace to talk about the upcoming transformation and learn which breast and nipple combination Ladda had selected. Denis, Joker, and I knew enough Thai to understand a little of the conversation.

Joker dimmed the lights. While we couldn't penetrate the deeper meaning of the chatter, we could spy on the body language. "Little Lek," Joker said, "is almost in tears."

What a true observation. Of the four women on the terrace, two had cleavage. In a few days, a third would join the ranks.

I wondered if Little Lek shared the same dream as Ladda.

During the dinner feast prepared by Suzy with the assistance of both Leks, Joker inquired about the expense of the breast enhancement.

"Fifty thousand baht at the clinic in my neighborhood," Denis said.

Suzy commented that Ladda's teacher's salary was too meager. Ladda, one of three Thai teachers of English in a private school, earned just 7,000 baht monthly.

"The good news," Denis said, "is that I just received eighty thousand baht in royalties from my two songs in *Bridget Jones's Diary.*"

The windfall enabled Denis to pay for the surgery. We toasted Denis for his triumph.

"My God," Suzy said, "she'll be indebted to you for life."

"Little Lek," Joker said, "you want big breasts?"

"I get one big and keep one small," she said, giggling as she covered her mouth.

Her wit made a positive impression on me.

Joker made the suggestion that there is a cosmetic way to display cleavage. No surgery needed. Little Lek listened attentively. Denis ran the idea by Ladda. They withdrew to the terrace for a discussion. Upon returning, Denis said Ladda would rather have real cleavage.

After dinner and more egg-nog—non-alcoholic, except for the brandy that Denis poured into his, mine, and Big Lek's glasses—

Joker turned on the music. In his heyday, Joker was a master jitterbug dancer. He gave private lessons to celebs like Steve Allen and his wife, Jane Meadows, at the famed Coconut Grove nightclub in Hollywood, which was owned by Merv Griffin, the host of *The Merv Griffin Show*. Joker performed on *The Steve Allen Show* and used to hang out at the Coconut Grove with the likes of Hugh Hefner, Merv, the Steve Allens, and Groucho Marx. I also saw Joker pictured with the actor Robert Duvall.

Joker hung out at the Coconut Grove until the club closed its doors in 2000. In Paris, the City of Lights, he and his partner, Jean Shelton, performed at top venues including the trendy Le Slow Club. The Slow is anything but slow. The dancers are fast-paced and come from all over Europe to make merry in the 'underground cave.' It has a medieval vaulted ceiling. Also performing at the celebrated Slow were legendary dancers like the Nicholas brothers, Fayard and Harold. At Joker's birthday party in San Francisco in 2003, another legendary dancer came to pay his respects and join in the fun. It was Frankie Manning, who continues to dazzle us with his unbelievable patterns in the swing dance known as the Lindy Hop. Another friend of Joker is Obba Babnatunde, the young jazz and tap dancer, singer, and film actor. Joker was also a dance consultant for several Hollywood movies.

One aerial specialty of Joker's was to stand behind Jean Shelton— she was five feet six inches—hold onto her shoulders, and catapult himself over her body; while in mid-air, he did a spread-eagle splits and then landed in a side-splits. At this party in 2004, on his sixtieth birthday, Joker did both versions of the splits. While he did not catapult himself over Little Lek, he showed us he was still as flexible and agile as a teenaged girl.

"I can do," Little Lek said.

"Do what?" Joker asked.

"Lek means that she can do the splits," Suzy said,

"Okay Lek, you talked the talk, now walk the walk."

Apparently the expression was unfamiliar. But she figured out the meaning and executed both versions of the splits. Done without effort. Done with ease and joy.

I asked Joker to show me some dip patterns and a "baby lift" that I could do with Little Lek. She brightened up even more at this thought. Joker trained me in sweeping Little Lek off her feet.

Afterwards, both Leks gave me a foot massage that included the calves, thighs, shoulders, neck, and head. Thumbs up to Big and Little. But I could not coax Big Lek into taking dance steps. Too shy.

Both were typically Thai—soft-spoken, polite, happy to serve guests at the dinner table, fix coffee, and demonstrate warmth. In terms of sense of humor, imagination, dance fever, ability to communicate in English—all this was in Little Lek's favor. Her boyish figure and girlish manner of covering her face when she laughed or giggled was charming. And she talked in 'triple rhythm.' For example: "I dance dance dance."

"For you, Richard, I cook cook cook."

"What else will you do for me, Little Lek?"

"I take care you. For sure."

"What does taking care of me include?"

She giggled and covered her face. "You think naughty. I know."

The final test was to determine who possessed the 'inner smile.' Some people refer to the inner smile as 'good vibes,' a 'charming personality,' or a 'good heart.' For me, the inner smile is a combination of all three, plus playfulness.

I played merengue music from a CD I brought with me. Big Lek politely declined, but Little Lek continued to be a good sport, and she picked up some of the merengue patterns easily. Little Lek also proved easy to lead in some salsa steps.

On that fateful night of Joker John's party, my choice between Little Lek and Big Lek could have been put on hold until I went out several times with both of them. That's what Suzy suggested. There was merit in the thought. There was feminine wisdom in the thought.

While mulling the matter over, the 'Heart Test' surfaced to my awareness. It posed the question: 'Which Lek has the laughing heart?'

Within seconds, the answer surfaced—Lek the Little.

I realized that her heart overflowed with laughter. In fact, she seemed to be embarrassed by her excessive happiness. She tried to hide it by covering her face. That, of course, made her more appealing.

After the dancing, Denis said that he and Ladda were ready to depart.

Suzy and Ying blocked the door. They told Denis and Ladda that they must sing Christmas carols before leaving. It's fun to hear Thais singing "Jingle Bells" and "Jingle Bell Rock"—which comes out as 'Jing-un Ben Lock.'

Bill Haley's "Rock Around The Clock" comes out as 'Lock Aloun' The Cock.'

It's a delight to hear Thais say 'Christmas': 'Kiss-ah-miss.'

During my version of "I Saw Mama Kissing Santa Claus," a momentous event occurred. Little Lek and Ladda were attacked by a fly. The prayer I had intoned earlier was being answered.

"Joker will kill the fly," I said.

Taking the cue, Joker blew his imaginary trumpet and began searching for the invader with his eyes.

"When the fly lands on the mirrored wall," I said, "Joker will swat it dead."

Little Lek heard the fly buzzing around her head.

"Don't try to swat it," Joker said. "I'll get it when it lands."

"Cannot see fly flying," Little Lek said.

"Impossible to see fly flying," Ladda agreed.

"He can," Suzy said. "I've seen it many times. Fly will fly no more when Joker wants it dead."

Both Leks, Ladda, and Denis were skeptical.

"Okay, Joker, show rather than tell," I said.

We sat on cushions in a semi-circle on the parquet floor, waiting for a fly to land on someone. Little Lek pointed to her face. We saw the fly taking a break on her cheek. Joker gestured that she try to kill it. The fly escaped unharmed, of course. All eyes were riveted on Joker as he 'watched' the fly's flight pattern.

"Look over there," he said, pointing to a spot on the full-length wall mirror. We looked, but found it difficult to believe. The fly was hanging out at that very spot.

"Lucky guess," Denis said.

"If all of you are quiet," Joker said. "I'll mosey on over there and have the fly fly away. While it's in flight, I will snatch it out of the air, choke it to death, and show you the remains."

"Ugly talk," Little Lek said. "I not watch. I go toilet."

Before departing, she asked if I would like a beer or egg-nog. I smiled and handed her my glass that was emptied of egg-nog. She took it with her.

During her absence, Joker snagged not one, not two, but three flies in flight. This was a feat that should be verified by the Guinness people and filmed by 'nano-second' cameras. (Later, I did write a letter to the Guinness headquarters, telling them what we saw. I asked if this unusual feat had been accomplished before. If not, would they like to investigate Joker John's remarkable eyesight and eye-hand co-ordination? Alas, no response.)

◆

Two days after Christmas, Little Lek met me at a Thai restaurant on Sukhumvit. After dinner, I asked if she would like to go to my place and practice some salsa patterns.

"Cannot see man alone in house."

But she responded to my disappointment with, "You want go Lek's house?"

We took a bus to the Impact shopping plaza, and then a *songtaew* (a pick-up truck 'bus' with two benches riveted to the bed) to a complex of twenty or so high-rise buildings. Her studio apartment was in one of those buildings. I expected to see her mother and brother or some other member of the family waiting to greet us. If not a family member, then one of her female friends. To my delight, her one-bedroom apartment was empty of people, but full of furnishings. The curtain to her bedroom was open. I could see the bed. Stuffed animals of all kinds were sprawled everywhere—teddy bears, cats, dogs, a pig, and a panda that was almost life size. I could see Lek snuggling up every night with all her friends. We played my salsa and cha-cha CDs and practiced both dances. In the dips, we got kissing close. We also worked on the lifts and tosses. It was effortless to lift and toss Little Lek.

She asked if I wanted to see her family album. I was curious about Choo, her ex-husband. He was a handsome lad. By the end of the third year of their marriage, Lek could not take any more of his coming home drunk and beating her. If he wasn't drinking the deadly Mekhong, he would be with other women. His drinking led to him losing his job as a construction laborer. He kept emptying their joint bank account. Lek took action by changing the lock of the apartment (which was in her name). She had to endure several months of him banging on the door to let him in. His disturbance disturbed the neighbors, who called the police. His downfall occurred when he fought the officers. He was put in jail for a month.

I saw pictures of Lek with trophies in high school for winning 100-, 500-, and 1,000-meter events. She showed me pictures of her in various yoga positions, including the full lotus. She showed me pictures of her wearing a hard hat in construction jobs. She had hurt her back and been unable to return to that type of work.

I spent the night with Lek, a true artist in bed. That's when I dubbed her "Lek Lick."

A week later, at her place, Lek told me the bad news: that her job as a foot massager had come to an abrupt halt. The owner of the beauty parlor where she worked had not paid rent for three months. As a result, the shop was closed down. Lek was thinking about going back to construction work and washing cars in her spare time. I asked her why she didn't seek work in another massage parlor; there is certainly no shortage of them in Bangkok.

"Foot massage all day hard work."

Her dream was to attend beauty school to learn hair styling. I gave her the tuition money—5,000 baht for three months of schooling. When she finished the course, I gave her another 5,000 to complete the advanced level.

I also decided to give her 5,000 baht every month.

◆

Tom, my friend in Saranjai Mansion, watched Lek's behavior at the swimming pool one weekend. She had prepared a tasty lunch and carried it down to the pool. She went upstairs and came back with a can of Cheers beer. In a thermos jug was hot coffee. She took care of us in true Thai style.

The next day, Tom again observed her in action. When she was in the pool, he came over and said, "That girl is devoted to you."

Dale, another friend (who had defended Bobby Fischer, the chess champion, in a *pro bono* case), made the same observation when he came to my place for dinner prepared by Lek.

When Lek and I went to La Rueda for salsa dancing, she would massage my back when I rested after spending time on the floor with her or other partners.

Lek and I often practice yoga together. In our partnering exercises, one of the patterns reminded me of rowing a boat. We sit opposite each other on the floor of my place, our feet and hands joined together. We alternate between her pulling away from me, making me stretch forward, and me pulling her towards me. This lengthens the muscles, tendons, and ligaments from the feet to the head. It creates freedom and mobility. The sciatic nerves are stretched and posture is improved. In addition, it soothes the muscles and stills the mind. One night, as we did this, I sang the song:

"Row, row, row, the boat,

"Gently down the stream,

"Merrily, merrily, merrily, merrily,

"Life is just a dream."

Lek liked the tune. While we pushed and pulled, I sang it again. Then she delivered her version:

"Load load load boat,

"Gently down *teem*,

"Mem-oh-wee, mem-oh-wee, mem-oh-wee,

"Life just I *deem*."

"Very good, Lek," I said. "Your voice is delicious."

"But my words very bad."

"Doesn't matter. I like your singing. Besides, your version is more colorful."

◆

In December 2005, I decided to tell Lek that I would be going to Cambodia to see Sweetpea, a 22-year-old Khmer girl I had met in Phnom Penh before I started dating Lek.

Sweetpea worked at the reception desk of the hotel I had stayed at in the Cambodian capital. She had been six months shy of graduating from college. I had spoken to her on several occasions during my week-long visit. Her command of English had startled me, as had her beauty and graceful demeanor. Sweetpea and I exchanged e-mails and I learned that she was now working for the Cambodian government. I kept telling her that I would be visiting her soon. She said she would be my tour guide.

It was almost one year since Lek and I had become intoxicated with each other. As much as I enjoyed Lek, I also wanted to continue my relationship with Sweetpea. I decided that I had to tell Lek I'd be going to Cambodia to see Sweetpea.

I sent Lek an SMS message that I would be going to Cambodia. The message was sent on a Monday. By Tuesday, I had received no SMS or telephone response from Lek. Perhaps she had decided to talk about the matter when she came over on Wednesday.

I was at the computer when Lek crept up behind me on the Wednesday evening. She tousled my hair and kissed me on the cheek. What a loving response!

Was she going to question me after the kiss, or was it up to me to bring up Sweetpea?

As usual, I was naked. I took Lek into the bedroom, where she took off her jeans to get comfortable. Unlike me, she would never be bare on top or bottom. "Not Thai," she had explained when I tried to coax her into nudity.

I followed her back into the kitchen. She unpacked groceries for dinner and asked if I was hungry. She began peeling potatoes.

"Lek Lick, I'm going to Cambodia to see my girlfriend."

She nodded. At the sink, she washed some of my favorite tropical vegetables and fruits.

"Honey, did you hear what I said?"

She turned to face me and stroked my face. She kissed me gently on the mouth, saying nothing. Action truly speaks louder than words.

"When you go Cambodia?"

"Maybe next week. Maybe the week after."

"I miss you when you go."

Her loving kindness was totally unexpected. I was happy that I did *not* have to explain that I loved her but was also attracted to other women. I did *not* have to explain that love, to me, meant not being owned by her. I did *not* have to explain that I believed in sex *with* love and sex *without* love.

Lek asked only one question about Sweetpea: "How old Khmer girl?"

"Twenty-two, honey."

She giggled when she said, "I know. You like young woman."

We spent that evening and the following night doing our yoga partnering and practicing tango patterns. She gave me a haircut, massaged me, cleaned the house, washed my clothes, the bed sheets and towels, scrubbed the bathroom floor after mopping the apartment, cooked my favorite Thai dishes, and said in bed, "I eat you."

I kept putting off Sweetpea because, as of this writing, I remain enamored with Lek.

And I finally figured out how to answer the candid comment made by Mikey, Lek's brother-in-law: "Richard, you are lucky to have a Thai girlfriend."

If I were to answer him now, it would be, "I know."

Massage Parlors

BOTH 'NAUGHTY' and 'nice' massage parlors co-exist on a peaceful basis in the Land of Smiles and carnal delight. Many of the naughty, and most of the nice massage girls receive their training from, and are certified by, the prestigious Wat Po in Bangkok. Another popular place for training in therapeutic massage is at the Ministry of Public Health complex, where classes consist of extensive history followed by a physical exam. The pocketbook does not take a hit. Bargain basement prices in Amazing Thailand.

The usual cost for a foot massage at either a naughty or nice establishment is a mere 200 baht an hour. The workout includes massaging the feet, calves, thighs, and, in some places, the neck, face, and head. Airports, department stores, and shopping centers have trained people who soothe the aching tootsies of travelers and shoppers. The old expression 'shop til you drop' is replaced by 'shop and then drop into a massage chair.'

My first ever massage in Bangkok was in October 2000. This was my maiden voyage to the magical kingdom. I had heard about traditional Thai massage, and the 'naughty' and 'nice' parlors. In the former, you could get a 'special massage'—a euphemism for carnal pleasure delivered by hand. That's what my friend Jim Platzek told me. Thanks to his ceaseless goading, I took the hint and came to the Land of Smiles, not realizing how much I was going to resonate with the Thai people and their culture. Instead of a cultural clash, I was immersed in a cultural cuddle.

Jim was somewhere in northern Thailand, on vacation with his new Thai girlfriend, Gop (Frog). I had met them both before they left for Chiang Mai and a trekking holiday to visit the hilltribe people.

Left to my own devices in Bangkok, I was passing the Friendly massage parlor and beauty salon, located on a *soi* off Sukhumvit Road near the Ambassador Hotel. A young woman, stylishly dressed, was blow-drying a lady customer's hair, and another worker was shampooing another female client. Three other women, clad in jeans and tight-fitting blouses, lounged in the foot-massage chairs, watching TV.

I walked past the place and then returned to take another look. Nervous about going inside, I strolled a few feet down the *soi*, careful not to step on the stray dogs snoozing in the late afternoon inferno. I turned around and made another trip to the parlor. I opened the *Bangkok Post*, pretending to read the front page; furtively, I glanced inside and caught the eye of a girl who wasn't watching TV. She smiled. I held the newspaper above my face, trying to hide.

"You like Thai massage, sir?"

Although I didn't see the face behind the seductive voice, I knew it was the one who wasn't watching TV.

Too nervous to respond, I pretended not to hear, and kept on 'reading.'

"Take your face from newspaper, shy man."

Once again, touched by a Thai. Seduction comes natural to them.

I had rehearsed what to ask—how much for a one-hour traditional Thai massage? But now, not only did I avoid looking at her, I was tongue-tied.

"I give good Thai massage, sir."

'I'm sure you do,' I said in my mind.

"Why you hide from Mouse? You more shy than I think." Gently, she took my hand and guided the newspaper down. Her touch was as soothing and soft as her voice.

"Er, do you do Thai massage?" I blundered. "Sorry, I mean that I would like a one-hour traditional Thai massage."

"Can do, sir."

She escorted me inside and sat me down in the chair she'd vacated. She excused herself, saying, "I come back one minute. You wait."

She returned and handed me a glass of cold water. In this heat, water, water, water.

"Very hot in Thailand," she said. "We have three weather here. Hot. Very hot. And more very hot."

I laughed.

She excused herself again and promised to return in two minutes.

Within three minutes, she had my shoes and socks off and my feet soaking in a big bowl of soothing cold water. 'Mouse' (that's what I thought I heard her say) then washed and wiped my feet with a towel.

"Very nice, Miss—"

"My name Mouse."

"Did you say 'Mouse'? My name is Mickey," I said. She squealed.

It was apparent that Mickey Mouse was well known in Thailand, as laughter erupted from Mouse, the hair stylists, and the customers.

"*Farang* funny," one of the customers said.

"How much for a traditional Thai massage?"

"Two hundred baht, sir. One hour. Very cheap, yes?"

A quick calculation—less than seven US dollars. "Yes, very cheap, Miss Mouse."

After bathing my feet a second time, Mouse toweled my tootsies, took my hand, and escorted me up a flight of stairs. Inside a dormitory-like room were ten mats spread out on the floor. She took me to the one in the corner and closed its curtains—like in a hospital ward—shutting off the world. She gave me loose-fitting pajamas.

I heard a rumble. Thank the Lord Buddha, it was the air conditioner. I was baking in this sizzling cauldron. She dimmed the lights, further shutting off the world.

Miss Mouse returned, clad in a toga robe. Sexy.

She went to work as I lay on my stomach. Her hands massaged my feet, then the ankles. By the time she was at my left thigh, both hands at work, I had figured out that a traditional Thai massage meant not touching the skin. What a gentle touch.

While Mouse wasn't a beauty, she had an elegance and charm that evoked lust. I tried to estimate the age of this raven-haired masseuse. Nineteen, twenty at most.

Instead of guessing her age, I ventured to ask.

"I thirty-two," she said. "How old you?"

"Sixty-four, Mouse."

She stopped massaging my left thigh and said something in Thai. Then she announced, in English, "Mouse think you 45."

"Thank you, Miss Mouse."

She had me turn over. Her hands moved higher and higher up my thigh, then to my waist. She untied the top of my pajama trousers and stared at my yearning member. I was embarrassed.

"Hair too long, sir. I cut, yes?"

I lifted my head and saw her tugging strands of my pubic hair.

"You want to cut *that* hair?"

"No extra cost, sir. Hair long very much." She excused herself.

During her absence, I indulged in fantasy. The fleeting images sent me into a state of rapture.

Miss Mouse reappeared with paper towels and a small pair of scissors. She turned up the light and went to work. When my schlong got in the way, she gently moved it to the other side. She asked me to stay still, fearful that I might be cut if I moved suddenly. I kept squirming, fantasizing, yearning. Finally she resolved the issue by literally taking the matter into her hand, by grasping the schlong and holding on to it while she deftly trimmed away.

What comes after the haircut? Perhaps it would be the 'special massage' my friend Jim had told me about. He warned me: "Be sure to negotiate the price." He advised me not to exceed 500 baht.

To my utter amazement, nothing. The trim done, she covered me up and proceeded with the traditional Thai massage.

When she indicated that one-hour was up, I gathered my courage, sat up on the mat, pointed to the schlong, and asked, "Mouse, do you do special massage?"

She giggled as she untied the pajama string. Then she pointed to the hallowed area and said, "You like special cut?"

"I like very much, Mouse. Can you do special massage?"

Then it dawned on her what I meant. She said, "Very sorry, Papa. Cannot."

She responded to my sorrowful gaze by writing on a business card. It was a name—"Lucky." Through body language and repeated talk, I understood that her friend, Lucky, was returning from holiday and would be in the parlor the next evening.

I tipped Mouse 200 baht, far in excess of the 25 percent that Jim suggested. She gave me a *wai* and kissed me on the cheek. Before I left, I inquired how she got her nickname. Her English was insufficient to explain. She told me that Lucky spoke good English and would be able to provide the information about her nickname.

"Papa be lucky with Lucky. She do special massage. For sure."

The next day, I walked into the Friendly massage parlor after the sun went down. Mouse and three women I hadn't seen the day before were watching the TV. I knew at once which of the three was Lucky. A long-haired beauty, she could have been 25, but looked sixteen. She was lighter in complexion than the others, including a woman having her hair styled. She wore cut-up jeans and a faded blouse. What she lacked in fashion sense didn't lessen my instant attraction to her.

Mouse jumped up, gave me a *wai*; so did Lucky. I *waied* back.

"Papa," Lucky purred. "I give you oil massage, okay?"

I asked what's the difference between traditional Thai and oil massage.

"No clothes on."

I smiled.

We discussed the price. One hour was a mere 400 baht.

Lucky asked to be excused to get water to wash my feet.

"Before you go, can you tell me how Mouse got her name?"

The women talked in Thai. Then Lucky turned to me. "Mother of Mouse nearly die when she see Mouse first time."

Lucky had the makings of a good storyteller.

"Mother of Mouse say unbelievable how little baby is."

"I thought all Thai babies were little," I said.

"But no Thai baby small like Mouse."

I told Lucky I knew how she got her own nickname.

"You not know that unless Mouse tell you." She turned to Mouse and learned that I hadn't actually been informed.

She waited for my guess, curious. All the others were in rapt attention.

"Your father won the lottery."

Lucky, after recovering from her astonishment, translated. The girls applauded.

"How you know that, Papa?"

"A lucky guess."

"Guess how much my papa won in lottery."

I shook my head, indicating I had no idea.

"Guess, maybe you be lucky two time."

A number popped into my head. I said, "Ten thousand baht."

Lucky, after recovering from her astonishment a second time, translated. The group applauded again.

"How you know this?"

"Another lucky guess."

The woman getting her hair done made a comment. The stylist and massage workers grimaced, as though in pain.

"What did she say?" I asked.

"In English, you have gift of sixth sense."

"My gift is *sex* sense."

When Lucky translated, instant howls.

"I give Papa extra special massage."

After the foot bath, I was escorted to a private room. A massage table contained a cut-out hole for the face as the 'patient' lay face down. I was told to take off my clothes. Lucky would return shortly. I kept my shorts on and was lying on my stomach when she entered.

"All clothes off, Papa," she said.

I was about to strip when she eased me out of my shorts. Embarrassed, I lay on my stomach.

"Lucky want to see haircut Mouse give yesterday."

I turned over, allowing her to get a quick glance at Miss Mouse's handiwork. Then I got back on my stomach.

"Papa, why you shy?"

Without waiting for a reply, she helped me turn; the front of my body faced her. Her fingers wove through the former bush. Her free hand stroked my abdomen, then moved south to join the engaged hand. "I see Papa maybe want special massage first. You want I take off my shirt?"

I nodded.

"You want I take off jeans?"

"Good idea."

There she was, wearing only hot pink panties. I was about to help her remove them when she said, "You give me one thousand baht for special massage. Yes?"

Jim had advised me to negotiate the price before giving the go-ahead. A quick calculation revealed the amount was 25 US dollars. If she had said a hundred US dollars, I would have agreed. I was in her power.

When playtime ended, Lucky had me lie on my stomach. She applied aromatic oil and rubbed my back, then my shoulders. She concentrated on the right shoulder, as though knowing the muscles were tight. She located a painful spot on the left side of my neck. After finding a third painful place, I realized she had a terrific talent.

"Papa, only safe place on you is—"

She took hold of my schlong and tickled it. When arousal became obvious, Lucky shouted in a voice loud enough to be heard in the salon.

Within seconds, the hair stylist and three other masseuses entered the room. Mouse was not among them. Lucky pushed her hair back with one hand as the other hand engaged in the 'special.' She spoke in Thai as the four women gathered on both sides of me. They were in wonder.

I guessed that Lucky had told them that she had played with me before and that I obviously yearned for more. One of the girls posed a question to Lucky.

Lucky translated. "You take Viagra, yes?"

"Never."

"Papa strong bull," was the reply.

◆

When Jim returned from his holiday with Frog, I told him about the extraordinary experiences in the Friendly massage parlor.

"From now on, don't pay more than five hundred baht."

To my surprise, Lucky agreed to the lower price the next time I visited. To prove there were no bad feelings, she undressed, then dimmed the lights. She placed my hand on her breasts. Then she lowered my hand to her bush.

"Can play my *nom* and pussy," she said. "You special customer."

Lucky: a carnal artist. I love Thailand too much.

But on my next jaunt to the Friendly massage parlor, I found that Lucky was on the resort isle of Koh Samui. She was enjoying the surf, sand, and sea with her newfound lover, a Frenchman.

"How long will she be on holiday?" I asked.

One of the hair stylists said, "Long time. She and Farangcet [French] boyfriend love."

Since I enjoyed Mouse's technique of using her hands, elbows, knuckles, knees, feet (and entire body when she gingerly walked on my back and legs), I had a two-hour traditional Thai massage. For two wonderful hours, Mouse rag-dolled me.

On the day before my departure for San Francisco, Miss Mouse suggested that I consider having Meow, an occasional worker, give me an oil massage. Mouse winked at me when she said, "Meow give good special. For sure."

"Miss Meow's special is better than Lucky?"

"Same but not same."

The next day, I surveyed three of the women watching the TV. None of them made a move toward me. Miss Mouse held up five fingers, indicating that Meow would be here very shortly. I lounged in the chair, waiting and watching the passing parade, when in strolled a young woman dressed to kill. Her black evening dress had spaghetti straps and a revealing slit.

A strange thing occurred when the mystery woman faced Mouse and the others. The hairdresser stopped cutting and the three workers stood up and *waied*. When the *wai* was returned, all resumed what they were doing.

I thought that this VIP was a fashion model, actress, or singer who came to have her hair styled in a modest salon. But no. She came directly to me. Her sweet smile seduced me as she *waied* and said, "You must be Richard, the gentleman with the sixth sense. And word has it you're a comic like Billy Crystal and Robin Williams."

My immediate reaction was—what a marvelous command of the English language by this exotic woman.

I qickly stood up to greet her and shake hands. When flesh met flesh, an electrical charge pulsed through my body. She generated power.

"Why do you see me as a comic?" I asked.

"They told me your talent includes what Thai people love—*phut len*. It means 'word play' and includes joking and teasing."

"You're referring to '*sex* sense'?"

She applauded and then said, "See. You made a play with words. Instead of 'sixth sense,' you bubbled up '*sex* sense.'"

What a whirlwind introduction. Her command of English continued to astound me. Not only was she the embodiment of erotica and beauty, she was also intelligent, imaginative.

Then I noticed the glimmer from her gold necklace, the glow from a gold bracelet on her right wrist and a gold anklet caressing her right foot. Her black, patent leather shoes also sparkled.

I became more intrigued.

Mouse brought Meow a bowl of warm water to bathe me. That made another impression on me. She didn't have to fetch the water

Why was she treated like royalty? Who would do the foot bath—Mouse or Meow?

To my surprise, Meow, not Mouse, took off my sandals and socks and began the bath. During this process, one of the girls served hot green tea to Meow and me.

The entire staff devoted their attention to Meow's method of cleansing and caring for the customer's feet. Chatting and watching the TV soaps ceased. That too, made me wonder how a seventeen- or eighteen-year-old was able to mesmerize the experienced hands.

The foot ritual over, Meow walked behind me as I climbed the stairs to the private room.

On the stairway, she goosed me and grinned.

"You like to be goosed, Mr. Richard?"

"By you, any time."

She dimmed the light when we entered the private room. I expected her to depart while I undressed. Instead, she took out a small designer duffel bag from under the table and withdrew a hot pink halter and short shorts. Not in the least bit shy, she took off her dress and released her bra. She slipped out of her see-thru laced panties.

I sat on the table, entranced.

She pointed to her heavenly haven. She was without bush. Totally bald. Since the room was dimly lit, perhaps I was imagining that she was *sans* pubic hair.

As if reading my mind, she turned the light up. In a teasing manner, her back faced me. She simulated a catwalk stroll, then turned around and stopped in front of me. She pointed to her treasure and said, "This is my young-girl look."

She opened her legs slightly. "Not one pubic hair," she said. "Take a look."

I got off the massage table and lowered my head to paradise. Not a single strand of hair.

"You like my young-girl look?"

"Lovely to gawk at, Miss Baldy."

My remark caused a howl. "Very funny, Mr. Richard. Very, very funny."

My face remained face to face with her non-bush. She said, "I can give you a young-boy look."

Instantly, I caught the meaning and raised my head. She mentioned that Mouse had given me an adolescent boy's look.

With no fuss or fanfare, she assured me it would take less than an hour for the transformation. No cutting or razor was involved. She showed me a cream and spatula she withdrew from her bag.

She helped me undress, eased me onto the table. I tried to turn onto my stomach, but she indicated that I stay front-side up. As she applied scented oil, her bubbly breasts occasionally brushed me. From the chest, she worked her way to my stomach, then the hips. She avoided touching the torch that was fully flamed. She paused and gave a look that said 'Mouse did a good job.'

I asked if she intended to make me into a young boy now.

Not possible. Tomorrow night she would come to my room.

"Meow, my plane leaves for San Francisco early in the morning. This is my last night in Thailand."

She slapped my schlong in a playful manner.

I remembered Jim's warning about agreeing on a price. "Miss Meow, how much for everything?"

"For you, only 800 baht."

"Okay," I said, not wanting to get stuck in a messy negotiation.

"With a generous tip, it comes to 2,000 baht. Not cheap, right?"

I loved her being so straightforward.

"Mouse told me Mr. Richard said, 'I love Thailand too much.'"

"My first visit this time was for a month. Now that I know I love Thailand too much, I'll return in three months and stay longer."

I asked if she could do me tonight.

"Sorry, cannot Mr. Richard."

"A previous engagement?" I asked.

"Yes."

Her hands caressed my inner thigh. She 'accidently' re-ignited the flame that had become an ember. She stood away from the table and turned my head to see her honey-colored body that glistened in the semi-darkness. She moved my hand to 'Miss Baldy.' I tried to squirm a finger within, but she gently took my hand and moved it to her breasts.

"Would Mr. Richard like to kiss one breast and play with the other one?"

Without answering, my tongue was soon afire from kissing her breast. She resumed stroking my schlong. Within a minute, she succeeded in creating a volcanic eruption.

She wiped me off with some packaged hand towels, and applied oil to my feet and calves.

She wanted to know what I thought about sex workers in America and how they differed from their Thai counterparts. I told her that my only experience was in a bordello outside Reno. It had seemed like a business transaction. Nothing more. Hardly was a word exchanged. The girl had a dour look.

I mentioned the film *Taxi Driver*, where Jodie Foster, playing a prostitute, took Robert De Niro to a hotel room for sex—

Meow looked at her watch and said, "the clock has started." Having quoted Jodie Foster's line, she added, "American girl very cold and always in a hurry."

I agreed.

"A Thai girl is trained to take care of a man," Meow said, as her hand searched for my schlong again.

She stroked softly, then with vigor, and softly again. I fondled her breasts and searched for Miss Baldy. This time she let me tickle her divine organ, but the finger was not allowed inside.

Another 'big O.' Another playful wiping. She sat me up and asked if I knew who Ramakrishna was.

"Yes, a big-time Indian holy man with remarkable powers."

"Do you know Ramakrishna's comment on prostitutes?" she asked.

"Yes, he saw prostitutes' work as being holy and divinely inspired. Because—"

Interrupting me, she said, "Because they make men happy."

That evening, I had dinner with Jim while Frog was visiting friends. I told him about the mysterious Meow and asked him if he could play detective and find out who she was, why she received royal treatment from the staff, and, if possible, how a youth of eighteen— her actual age—became so expert in naughty massaging and was so worldly.

◆

One paradox that is part and parcel of Thailand is that there are massage parlors that *do not* give massages.

My friend Alex once introduced me to these glitzy 'massage' palaces that resemble Las Vegas casinos. Many are located in the Ratchadapisek section of Bangkok. The parking lots outside these establishments accommodate hundreds of vehicles including private cars and luxury tourist buses containing visitors from many nations. Taxis deposit men into the stadium-sized lots. Much walk-in traffic is another aspect.

Alex took me into the posh lobby of one such emporium. Behind glass windows were young women in cocktail dresses and formal evening gowns. They sat on rows of benches. Each wore a number on her gown. Their beauty and demeanor attracted me.

"Richard, before we sit down to enjoy the view," Alex said, "let's browse all of the fish bowls."

Alex took me on a tour of the 'bowls.'

"This place," he said, "has 'virgins.'"

'Virgin,' he explained, meant that this was their 'first day' on the job.

"Of course, many of the tourists believe that these girls are untouched. The price is around 2,000 baht. That includes the room upstairs, *boom-boom*, and a bath. It doesn't include drinks or her tip."

We sat at tables adjoining the bar. A scantily clad waitress came to take our order. Alex spoke in Thai. She nodded and walked away. One of the burly men dressed in a dark suit and tie came to our table and asked which girl pleased us. Alex told him in English that I was new in town and he was showing me around. The man wished me a pleasant stay and suggested we stay as long as we liked.

"Suppose I just wanted a massage?" I asked Alex.

"Not in this place."

◆

In Thailand, some of the naughty massage parlors have staff members who will not give 'special' massages to customers. The 'nice' girls may earn ten US dollars on a good day, which involves twelve to fourteen hours of work—or, more likely, sitting around waiting for customers. On a bad day, there are no customers at all. Since most of the girls work on a commission basis, there is no income on such days. Despite coming up empty, nice girls seldom work 'specials' to improve their earning capacity. To them, virtue is more important than money.

Many massage establishments offer free lodging for the workers. The masseuses sprawl out on mats in a dormitory room, usually located on the top floor. The ladies view this as an attractive perk. Another benefit is that some have a communal kitchen.

Those who give specials can make up to fifty US dollars a day, mostly from tips. Fifty dollars in Thailand is equivalent, in relative terms, to 300 in the USA. Seldom are there bad days for the naughty workers. One or two regular customers saunter in occasionally. Some of the naughties take care of those girls less fortunate by putting a portion of their earnings into a pool-sharing pot.

I asked my friends what they like about massage parlors. All agreed that this was the best way to have save sex. A 'special' massage involves hand sex. No intercourse. But another special is known as 'I smoke you.' This involves, to use another euphemism, a 'tongue bath.' Once again, no intercourse. Several friends told me they don't know what they'd do if there were no naughty massage parlors in the Land of Smiles.

Massage in Thailand provides pleasure galore, whether it is given to the feet, or whether it is traditional with loose-fitting garb. Pleasure is also achieved through oil or aroma massage, or a body scrub that includes a bath given by the masseuse. The upmarket health spas offer non-sexual body scrubs. After your body is scrubbed with a soft brush on the massage table, you get into a warm bath and are scrubbed again. Definitely no sexual favors in these places, but still an exhilarating experience.

The Bargirls And The Pendulum

THE SESSION took place in my apartment with the wrap-around terrace that overlooks the aquamarine swimming pool and the Bangkok cityscape. A delight to behold, Miss Oy, a beauty of slim proportions, told me through the interpreter, Jum, that her first sexual experience had been about eighteen months before.

Aged 21, the big event would have occurred when she was nineteen. I would have taken her for sixteen. She reported that she came from a small village near Udon Thani in northeastern Thailand. She reported that she hangs out at ATM machines near the Ambassador Hotel on Sukhumvit Road. When a foreigner has trouble operating the money machine, this Good Samaritan comes to the rescue. Most likely, the potential customer is new to the kingdom, meaning Oy can charge double for her service. But if he wants to bargain for a lower price, no problem. "I give discount if *farang* knows price," Oy said.

The following list shows the assorted places where a person can be picked up for carnal pleasure in Thailand. It is taken from the book, *Guns, Girls, Gambling, Ganga: Thailand's Illegal Economy And Public Policy*, published in 1998 by Pasuk Phongpaichit, Sungsidh Piriyarangsan, and Nualnoi Treerat: "Brothel, sauna, massage parlor [in the Bangkok Yellow Pages under "massage parlors" there are many listings offering 24-hour service to your hotel room or apartment], traditional massage parlor, garden restaurant, hotel, barber shop, teahouse, bungalow, membership club, cocktail lounge, karaoke club, pubs, beer bar, gay bar, go-go bar, *ramwong* bar, nightclub, coffee shop, discotheque, beauty parlor, telephone call [Bangkok Yellow Pages under "escort services"; hundreds of listings], streetwalker, other."

Of these categories, Oy's preference is 'other.' In this case, 'other' means ATM machines. She's clever in that she goes where the money is. On a rainy night, she hangs out in venues like the German beer garden on Sukhumvit Soi 7, the celebrated Thermae coffee shop, or the café in the cavernous Grace Hotel on Sukhumvit Soi 3.

After rescuing a hapless victim from the money machine, she asks if he would like to buy her a drink. "You save money. Me drink orange juice. Very cheap in Thailand."

The potential customer is usually curious at the double entendre. Does Oy mean that the drink is cheap or that she is available at a cheap price? Or both? Either way, this is going to be an inexpensive experience.

Relevant background 'facts': Oy's mother and father are rice farmers. She said that she has a younger brother she is putting through air traffic controller school in Bangkok; she has a younger sister in high school. The father's heavy drinking and philandering resulted in his poor health, including diabetes that is complicated with severe kidney problems. He had not worked for two years. Her mother sold lottery tickets and made lunch from her pushcart 'restaurant.' Annual family income—excluding Oy's more substantial contribution— is around 1,000 US dollars.

Oy has a sixth-grade education; her English-language skill is adequate to negotiate the price and entertain customers with quixotic bargirl sayings like 'I smoke you'; 'I take care you'; 'Tell me what you like and I do'; 'I cook good. I never dunk from dink.'

'You never what from *what*?'

The client learns that she is trying to say she may drink occasionally, but is never drunk. This endears him to her even more. He is unaware that it is seduction talk.

Oy lives in a one-room hovel in a low-rent district on the outskirts of Bangkok. She has no air conditioner and no refrigerator. Her weekly earnings average 5,000 baht. Most of it goes to put her brother through the air traffic controller school and his housing and food expenses. More goes to her mom and sister, with the stipulation that no funds are given to her father.

Oy said that she left her village two years before. She came to Bangkok and worked as a live-in maid for eighteen months.

"In that case," I said to my interpreter, "Oy has been practicing her trade for six months. Is that right?"

After the translation, it was confirmed that this '21-year-old' beauty had been in the sex industry for six months.

During the telling of her tale, Oy giggled often. At first, Jum felt uncomfortable. Then she began to laugh at some of Oy's remarks. Numerous times, both of them giggled in a delightful, girlish manner—a telltale sign that fabrication was the order of the day. When the appropriate time came, I would discover what was true and what was false. My ace in the hole, my *hammerschlagen* truth serum would take the form of a crystal pendulum.

Now that the relevant 'facts' were made, it was time to learn how much truth had been told. I took out my blue crystal pendulum at the end of its silver chain.

"What's that called?" Jum asked.

"A pendulum. Very popular in the USA, Canada, UK, Japan, and many European countries," I said.

Following established protocol, the counterweight at the top of the chain is grasped by the thumb and index finger. After gesturing to Jum and Oy, I asked for silence on the set. I held the pendulum in front of me, chest high.

"Jum, tell Oy that when the crystal swings side to side, it means 'no.' When it swings forward and backward, it means 'yes.'"

Jum did as instructed. Both were curious.

"Knowing Nose," I asked the pendulum, "Is Oy 21 years old?"

The pendulum pondered the question and began to vibrate. It moved sideways, indicating 'no.'

"It's saying that Oy is not 21."

Both girls looked at each other.

On a hunch (sniffing out the truth), I said, "Knowing Nose, is Oy seventeen years old?"

Knowing Nose 'listened' attentively and began to vibrate by swinging forward and backward.

"Jum, tell Oy that she has made a mistake. She's seventeen, not 21."

Oy's face froze. She was trying to mask an emotion.

I gave Jum the crystal and asked her to ask it a question.

"How old is Khun Richard?"

The pendulum remained silent. "See," Jum said, "it doesn't know."

When she translated the question to Oy, both chuckled.

"Jum, you must ask a question that requires a 'yes' or 'no' response. Try again."

"Is Richard 68 years old?"

Negative.

"Is Richard seventy years old?"

Negative.

"Is Richard 69 years old?"

A forward and back swing, indicating 'yes.'

Jum was beginning to be convinced. "Am I 31 years old?" she asked Knowing Nose.

Knowing Nose swung back and forth. Affirmative.

"Am I from Isaan?"

Knowing Nose swung side to side.

"Is Richard a ladyboy?"

I laughed as Knowing Nose swung side to side.

I held out my hand and received the pendulum. As I prepared to ask the next question, I noticed Oy squirm while Jum's eyes focused on the blue crystal.

"Knowing Nose, has Oy been practicing her trade—"

The pendulum began swinging wildly while I was in mid-sentence; back and forth it vibrated.

"—as a sex worker for *eighteen* months?"

Usually it swings a half inch, sometimes one inch. On this occasion it moved forward and back at least three inches.

"*Phii*!" Oy gasped. "*Phii*!" A ghost!

"Knowing Nose, has Oy been a sex worker more than three years?"

Affirmative.

"*Mor doo*!" Oy shouted. "*Mor doo*!" Fortune-teller! She thought that the crystal had a sixth sense. Desperate, she began to pace the living room.

"Knowing Nose, was Oy a virgin until eighteen months ago?"

Jum translated.

Oy fled onto the terrace when she observed Knowing Nose's answer as it vibrated side to side, creating a silent crescendo that reverberated in her heart. She had lost 'face.'

"Lord Buddha," Jum said. "How does Knowing Nose *know* these things?"

"I'll explain later," I said. "Meantime, calm her down."

"Okay, I take tissue with me. I think she need."

I watched the two of them on the terrace. Oy's back was to me. She was trembling. I fixed two martinis for Jum and me, and Oy's favorite wine cooler drink. On Jum's advice, I had stocked the fridge the day before.

Jum *waied* me and took the martini from the tray. She nodded to her friend with the loss of face to have her favorite drink. I served Oy's drink in a wine glass. Without looking at me, she *waied* and accepted.

"*Chai yo*," Jum said. Glasses clinked. I left them, went back inside, and played a Gypsy Kings album. Their festive flavor can ease people into a better mood.

When the two returned, I served Oy another wine cooler. Still uneasy, she avoided looking at me. She stared at Knowing Nose.

"She thinks a ghost in there," Jum said. "Can you put it away?"

Oy immediately melted into a sea of calmness when I tucked the 'ghost' into a drawer. Then she kept giggling as she told us why she likes her work.

"Little man," Oy said, pointing to my groin, "like flower. I tickle. It grow and grow. Little man grow to big big."

She downed the wine cooler and was given another by Jum, who prepared two more martinis, making hers a double with six olives.

"After *boom-boom*, little man fall over like flower and die."

She slurped her drink and became merrier. "After resting, I tickle and talk to little man. It wake up. First dead, then it grow and grow. I tickle more. It make me excited. Make me feel my power."

Oy made mouth movements, simulating a 'tongue bath.'

"Job very good me. Not work many hours like maid. Not have one day holiday every month, like maid. Make more money in two day than maid make six month."

"Do your parents know what kind of work you do?"

"They happy. Younger sister happy, too."

Strange, I thought. She didn't mention the younger brother she told us she was putting through air traffic controller school. I made the 'time-out' gesture. Jum told Oy that I would make use of 'ghost' again. I retrieved Knowing Nose and sat next to Oy. She was terrified.

"Knowing Nose," I began, "Does Oy have a brother—"

She gasped as her hand grasped Knowing Nose. "Sorry, Richard, I lie. Not have brother. Please put ghost to sleep."

I nodded and put ghost to sleep in the drawer again.

Relieved, Oy reported that the entire village was happy about her earning power. Through Oy's heroics, other young girls had come to the City of Angels to improve their and their family's economic problems. (In fact, I said to Jum, one of them, Tickle, might be my next subject. Seizing the moment, Jum took down Tickle's mobile number.)

"What about HIV and AIDS?"

"Much worry."

"Do you get tested?"

"Afraid to test."

But, Oy said, the way things were going, she would have enough of a bankroll to stop romance work in two more years. Then she intended to get vocational training in one of the Christian churches or an NGO agency that offered English-language study along with other educational programs. All free, thanks to the generous Christians and NGOs based in Thailand.

Her dream after she escaped from this line of work was to get a job in an Internet shop or somewhere she could meet "many *farang.*" Maybe even go to America or the UK and have a baby who would grow up speaking English. Or marry a Dane or German. Baby would still learn English.

It was nearing ten o'clock. The session had gone on five minutes short of three hours. Oy asked Jum something. Jum thought it was a good idea.

"Richard," Jum said, "Oy wants to know if the ghost knows which place will give her a customer tonight."

Oy wanted to know exactly where she could get a customer within fifteen minutes—the money machine, the beer garden on Soi 7, the Grace Hotel, or the cellar Thermae café.

Knowing Nose 'spoke' in the positive at the money machine and negative at the other establishments.

When Oy left, Jum pounced on me with a barrage of questions about the pendulum. How does it work? How accurate is it? Where does its power come from?

I told her about when the great inventor Thomas Edison was asked 'What is electricity?' He answered that he didn't know, but it sure worked. He focused on its uses.

Interesting, she mused, but not satisfying.

I asked what was on her mind.

She wanted to know about her relationship with her new boyfriend from the UK.

"Ask the pendulum if the two of you are good for each other."

"Good idea. I need to know that."

Try as she might, she could not hold her hand steady as she held the blue quartz crystal suspended on its silver chain.

"Would you like me to ask for you?"

"What? It knows about me and Alistair, even if you do it for me?"

"Correct. Knowing Nose knows, no matter who asks it."

She fidgeted as she watched me.

"Knowing Nose, is Alistair good for Jum?"

The pendulum was still, too still. Then it began to jerk in a haphazard manner. It seemed to be coughing and spewing in a most erratic way. With my hand, I quieted it, then repeated the question. The same result occurred.

"Ahhh, ghost not know. Is fake."

"Jum, you're not going like the answer."

I saw the fear in her eyes. "Ghost fake. It not say yes or no."

"Jum, do you and your boyfriend fight many times?"

She lowered her head, avoiding eye contact.

"Are you always arguing?"

Her head sunk lower.

I brought a box of tissues from the kitchen counter and placed them on the coffee table.

"Do you curse each other?"

The dam broke. She used many tissues.

I explained that the pendulum gyrated wildly because it was demonstrating, in a forceful way, that their relationship was stormy.

"Knowing Nose, is Jum the one who loves too much in this relationship?"

'Yes,' it spoke.

"Unbelievable," Jum said.

"The one who loves too much suffers more," I said.

Jum nodded.

I asked Jum if they had good sex.

"Very good. Best sex for me ever. He sex-crazy for me, too."

"Jum, let me put that question to Knowing Nose to confirm that what you said about Alistair is true.

"Knowing Nose, does Alistair agree that sex with Jum is very good?"

She waited for the response.

As Knowing Nose lurched back and forth, indicating total agreement, Jum shrieked—"Knowing Nose knows *everything*."

Her phone rang. From the excited exchange, I was able to tell that Oy was the caller. While they conversed, I asked Knowing Nose, "Did Oy get a customer already?"

'Yes.'

When Jum hung up, I told her that I had consulted with Knowing Nose and learned that Oy was excited because it was accurate again. By this time, Jum was totally in awe of the 'ghost's' ability to prophesize.

"Him best ghost ever," she said.

I introduced the idea of Jum changing her relationship with Alistair to a casual affair instead of being one of love.

"Richard, what you mean?"

I told her that they clashed emotionally, intellectually, and possibly spiritually. In bed, they clicked instead of clashed. She might consider talking to him about having only a sexual relationship—an affair.

Jum borrowed Knowing Nose to pose the question: "Mr. Knowing Nose, is better for me have good sex with Alistair instead of mean love from him?"

'Yes.'

"Please," she pleaded, "tell me more how Mr. Knowing Nose works."

I explained that the first documented evidence of such a device was Jacob's Rod in the Bible. Jacob used a forked wooden stick as a divining rod to find water in the desert. Later on, the rod used by Jacob evolved into what is known as the pendulum. It is said to pick up the inner energy (or force field) of the user; it also tunes in to the outer energy (the magnetic field), outside the body of the user. The device radiates sensitivity, which is the meaning of its Latin name—*radiesthesia*. In physics, it's known as 'relational physics,' or energy force fields.

Some medical professionals in the UK, Germany, France, and Russia recognize the value of the pendulum in healing, in relationships, in choosing a vocational career, and in making business decisions. Not so in the USA, where the medical profession frowns on its use as a diagnostic tool.

Jum was informed of another use of Knowing Nose. On my terrace are seven tropical plants and three tropical bushes. I asked her to find out which plant or bush needed water.

She filled up a water jug and proceeded to talk to the inanimate flora with her hand on the crystal that radiates sensitivity. I watched her from the living room as she watered one plant and one lush bush.

Jum came in, smiling, waving the crystal. She wanted to know how she could get one.

I explained that it is the invisible vibrations from the subject that make a pendulum work. An improvized pendulum could be made from a simple paper-clip chain and any kind of weight, like a key, at its end. However, a crystal from Mother Earth has more Power.

"No problem, Jum. I'll make you one tomorrow."

◆

A few days later, I met Tickle. A honey-toned woman, she bubbled with joy. Aged twenty, she looked thirteen, fourteen at the most. According to Knowing Nose, she spoke the truth about her age.

She reported to Jum that she had two younger brothers. She was putting one of them through the expensive air traffic controller school in Bangkok.

So, she was using the same story as Oy.

Jum coughed when she translated the air traffic controller yarn.

When I showed her Knowing Nose, Tickle tickled me in the ribs. I wasn't sure if she had been warned about the crystal's power. I tickled Tickle after she zeroed in on my ticklish spots on both sides of my body. That's when I found out she likes to tickle and be tickled.

I asked Knowing Nose if the tall tale about putting her brother through the air traffic controller school was true. When the pendulum swung side to side, indicating 'no,' Tickle was puzzled by my talking to the pendulum and its talking back. Apparently she had not been forewarned by Jum.

Jum told her that the crystal said she was *not* paying her brother's way. Furthermore, it was learned that Tickle had one *older* brother.

Tickle replied: "Ghost know I lie. So sorry."

What a refreshing way to admit that she had lied.

Since I am obsessed about the age that bargirls lose their virginity, the question was posed: "At what age did you stop being a virgin?"

Tickle wanted to put the query in a playful manner. "Ask ghost if I virgin one year already."

Nose sniffed out a 'no.'

"Was Tickle a virgin two years ago?"

'No.'

She held up three fingers.

'No.'

Tickle was thrilled with the uncanny accuracy of 'ghost.'

She held up four fingers.

Once again, 'no.'

Five fingers. Hmmm, that would have put her at age fifteen.

Not a virgin at fifteen was ghost's response.

"Knowing Nose, was Tickle a virgin at age fourteen?"

'No.'

"At age thirteen?"

She squealed when ghost responded with a resounding 'yes.' She did not want to discuss how she was introduced to sexuality at such an early age.

But I did.

It was learned that Bangkok is her hometown. As a schoolgirl (before high school), she and her friends were befriended by a beautiful, sexy, and intelligent woman. Tickle referred to her as "my mob mother."

Through Jum, I learned that the high-school girls looked upon 'mob mom' with reverence. They always gave her a special *wai*, as though honoring an exalted person.

Through the guidance of her mentor, Tickle began to frequent Banglamphu, the section of Bangkok where Western backpackers hang out. She and two friends picked up tourists for easy money. They wore T-shirts with the slogan on their chest: "Cheap But Good." On the back of the shirts, the same slogan in Thai: "*Took Dare Dee.*"

The three girls offered their combined services at the bargain-basement price of 2,000 baht. After sex at a guesthouse in Banglamphu, they partied with dinner and drinks on the customer, served in the room. Then, all the merry makers would go to a karaoke bar for singing. Once the girls got the hang of it, 'mob mom' introduced them to her friend who ran a "special place." Due to secrecy, this place was not specified. The trio's income rose. They didn't object to 'mob mom' getting a cut of the action.

At an early age, Tickle learned that making a living by lying down on the job was easy in the City of Angels. After three years in the business of freelancing, she discovered, through her mentor, that "I become virgin again."

"What!" Jum exclaimed.

"Is true. I become virgin again. Get high price in massage parlor on Ratchada."

At this point, she opened a photo album. I was dazzled by the glitzy and glamorous cocktail dresses she wore. The images were taken in front of the high-priced massage parlors and hotels in the Ratchadapisek district. In the cocktail lounges, she posed with Westerners in expensive biz suits, and rich visitors from the Middle East. It was obvious that they adored the 'born again virgin.'

Jum wanted to know from Knowing Nose if it was true that this young woman had regained her virginity.

The crystal wavered, unsure.

But there was no doubt about Tickle's answer—yes, she was a virgin, in the sense that she had what men all over the world crave for: "I have tight pussy again."

Jum wanted to know how this was accomplished.

So did I.

Tickle gave a detailed explanation to Jum, and I got the edited version.

Later, I asked Joker John about this. His American wife had become a 'virgin' again after the birth of their son. Just as in a face-lift, an incision is done, some tissue removed, and a tighter stitch made. A harmless, easy procedure. According to him, it is called the "hubby stitch." (In Japan, the procedure to become like a virgin is known as "surgical re-flowering.")

"My mob mom tell me how do," Tickle added.

"Her name, please," Jum pleaded.

But 'mob mom's' identity was a secret.

On a hunch, I asked Nose to sniff out the mysterious lady's name. "Is mob mom's first initial 'M'?" I asked.

Tickle cried out in anguish when Nose 'spoke' with force, indicating 'yes.'

"Is her name Meow?"

'Yes.'

"How you know Meow?" Tickle asked.

I told her that I'd had a feeling in the pit of my stomach when Tickle said that mob mom was treated like a royal personage. "Can you show me a picture of this Meow?"

"Sorry, she not want me take picture her."

What was of paramount concern to Jum was information about becoming a virgin again.

A heated conversation ensued. Both of them drank Cuba libres and clinked glasses. Jum grasped the blue crystal and spoke in a sweet tone. "Knowing Nose," she said, "can a woman who fucked many many times become a virgin again?"

The 'one' in contact with the cosmic answered 'yes.'

Smiling sweetly, Jum called for a toast. I poured more Cuba libres. Glasses clinked.

"I surprise Alistair," Jum said.

When we got back to the session, I asked Tickle, "What is your goal in life?"

Her answer was the standard one for bargirls. One: marry a rich or poor Westerner. Two: have children. Three: open her own Thai restaurant in the US or UK.

◆

When Jum introduced me to the next romance worker, a nickname came to mind—Sad Face. She reminded me of the character in Al Capp's cartoon strip, "Li'l Abner." It ran from 1934 to 1977 and equaled the popularity of "Peanuts."

In Sad Face, I was reminded of one of Al Capp's characters. It was Joe Btfsplk. Like Btfsplk, Sad Face carried a dark cloud over her head. Wherever Joe Btfsplk went, the cloud burst open and it rained on everybody's party. People saw Btfsplk coming and immediate action was taken. Abandon ship! No one was excited by the prospect of being entertained by 'Mr. Gloom an' Doom.'

Sad Face worked in a 'tongue bath' establishment. The 2006 price for 'bathing' the customer was 800 baht. Her take came to 600 baht per head, so to speak, plus a tip of 100 or 200 baht. If the customer bought her 'lady drinks,' she would earn forty baht for each of those. Her earnings were excellent, since she served two or three clients a day.

Sad Face was on the job six months. Prior to her 'good fortune,' she worked the street scene, where she was lucky to recruit three customers a week.

◆

The setting is a small village near Surin, in northeastern Thailand. Sad Face, dressed in a dark rag that passed for a dress, saw her father stumble and fall headfirst into the rice paddy water. She and Suwanna, her ten-year-old sister, came to his rescue. They pulled his head above the water. Her father maneuvered his head into her lap. She comforted him as best she could. She discovered that stroking his head and face soothed him.

"Father, this is the third time in a week that you've become dizzy and fallen into the water."

He smiled at her. When his hand, on its way up to her face, paused at her chest, the thirteen-year-old girl with budding breasts thought nothing of it. When he clawed at her nipple, she giggled, took his hand away, and said, "Father, that tickles."

"Help me up," he said.

The two girls sandwiched themselves between him and took him to dry land. He asked Sad Face to help him home and told Suwanna to look after the family's prized possession, Sat, the water buffalo.

At home, a hovel that was an inferno in the hot afternoon and a mosquito haven in the sizzling night, father seemed to have made a remarkable recovery. With his wife away until the sun went down, he seized this long-awaited moment. He showed a training bra to his teenaged daughter. When she realized it was a gift, she was ecstatic.

He asked her to try it on. Turning away from him, she placed the treasure across her chest. Unable to hook the clasp, she felt his hand on her back. With the bra secured, she lowered the dirty cloth that served as her only dress and faced him. He placed a small mirror in front of her. With the bra on, she viewed herself in a woman's body.

"False bra makes you look big on both sides," Father said. "Next year, you'll not need a training bra. I'll get you better one."

Spellbound, she gazed at herself, proud at the sight.

"Now," Father said, "put this on."

He handed her a pair of black lace, see-through panties. She had never seen anything like it.

Putting the mirror down, she turned away and eased into the panties. When she faced him, he lifted the dress above her chest. Not knowing what to do, she stood before her father. In the next moment, the old dress was on the floor. He gazed at the sad-faced girl of thirteen. He unzipped the bra and lowered the panties until they too, dropped to the earthen floor.

He lowered his pants and guided her head down. He showed her how he liked to be licked; how he liked to be touched, tasted, fondled, and stroked gently after the "big explosion."

A year she continued to be his sex toy. Sad Face was convinced that her mother was aware, but she said nothing.

In the second year, Sad Face noticed that her sister, now twelve, had also become sad and lifeless.

"How long has Father been inside you?"

Younger sister did not answer.

"How long? One month? Two months?"

"Two weeks already."

◆

Thanks to Sad Face's going into the sex trade, her younger sister was no longer at the mercy of her father's passion.

Every month, Sad Face returned home with cash for her mother, gifts for her younger sister, and presents for Father—three bottles of Mekhong. Before departing for Bangkok, she stockpiled the house with a dozen more bottles of the brew that is more toxic to the liver and brain than the imported varieties. Her father partied and drank with his friends, who viewed him as a lord.

Like an increasing number of Thais, her father was a diabetic. Drinking the deadly Mekhong accelerated the diabetes and caused extensive damage to other vital organs. The power of the libido was gone. His condition caused acidosis attacks that required longer periods of hospitalization.

Life in the house without her father was characterized not so much by joyous celebration, but by something equally important—contentment.

Sad Face earned enough to provide good hospital care. Once, when she visited him in hospital, she saw that her power had overwhelmed him. The weaker he became, the happier she was. The emaciated figure could no longer walk and barely talk.

"You take good care of me," her father managed to say from his sickbed when she withdrew a silver flask from her purse and held it to his mouth. He guzzled the Mekhong with zest.

Her father was dead six months later. Instead of being happy at his demise, she felt remorse for having taken a life. "Is big sin for Buddhist" she moaned to me in the presence of Jum.

I took out the pendulum and asked her to watch the way it answered a question I was about to pose.

"Knowing Nose, does Sad Face's father forgive her?"

I knew what the answer would be because I had rehearsed it during a bathroom break.

'Yes.'

For the first time, I saw Sad Face smile. It was followed by tears of joy. Jum held one hand; I held the other.

◆

I was having afternoon drinks with two friends in the lobby bar of Pattaya's Diana Inn. George, a Japanese-American from San Francisco, was telling us about a fellow American he had met a week ago. "The dude," George said, "had not experienced pleasure with a woman for *thirty-plus* years."

At the persistence of his best friend, Dude had decided to find out for himself that "the harlots in Thailand don't give a fuck how old you are."

George went on to say, "The dude in question has a tire belly, dresses poorly, is 57, and not at all good looking."

George's buddy, Abe Hoffman, also from San Francisco, agreed with his friend's assessment.

It was obvious that the picture they painted was a dude of multiple imperfections.

George answered his mobile phone. . . . "Okay, see you in five. We're having drinks in the lobby."

George held up five fingers. "Richard, in five minutes, you'll see the tire-bellied, fashion-challenged, ugly-as-can-be Dude."

George was right. Dude bounced to our table, gushing with glee. He wore plaid Bermuda shorts; his belly drooped over the belt. His Hawaiian shirt clashed with the shorts. His hairstyle created a comic effect, as it was obvious he wore a toupee. Dude ordered a round of drinks for us. His choice was Pimm's Cup Number Seven with three slices of cucumber.

Dude was a bowling ball with legs. "I want to tell you about my Thai jewel," he said. "She's a dream doll. An all-day fucker and an all-day sucker."

He stopped talking and took to gawking. A woman of extraordinary beauty that matched her extraordinary body approached us.

"Isn't she the cat's meow," Dude said, slobbering.

Standing beside him was none other than Meow, the stunning and glamorous woman I had met in the Bangkok massage parlor three years before. She recognized me immediately and called me by my Thai name, Muu Waan (Sweet Pig).

Without hesitation, Meow told everyone how she met me when she worked in the massage parlor. She asked if I still had my hair "trimmed down there."

"Meow, I'm happy to report I'm bald there. I found someone who knew how," I said.

The waitress brought her a Pimm's Cup Number Seven with three slices of cucumber. Meow and Dude clinked glasses. The Dude drooled. Meow's mere presence electrified him above and below. She began tousling his toupee until it came loose. Like a scalp, she held it high for all to see.

Dude, speechless, blushed. She placed the toupee back on his head, making sure it was on backwards. She giggled, tickled his paunch, then took out a mirror and showed him how he looked in his now-rumpled wig.

Meow roared with delight at the spectacle. Seeing her merriment, Dude joined her in laughter, as did all at the table and the patrons and bar staff.

Gazing at himself in the mirror, Dude said, "The cat's Meow! I'll wear it this way from now on!"

She rubbed his tummy, then his cheeks, causing more drooling. She wiped his mouth with a napkin, pleasing Dude. She placed the napkin on his lap and gave him a baby tickle you know where. More drooling.

"I tell you," he purred, "they don't give a fuck how old we are. Or how fat we are."

"But she's charging you five times the going amount," George protested.

"Relax, George, I know."

"What do you mean, 'you know'?"

"The cat's Meow told me she's charging me too much. I like that kind of honesty."

"You my big fat honey," she said in her 'bargirl English,' blowing into his ear, making him gush again.

"You know what else the cat's Meow told me?"

"Is it inside info on Thai women?" I asked.

"Why yes," Dude said. "How did you know?"

"A lucky guess," I said.

I remembered what George had told me before Dude's and Meow's arrival. Dude had not experienced pleasure with a woman for thirty-plus years. From sexual famine in the USA to a sexual feast in tasty Thailand, Dude was in a state of perpetual drool that was now mixed with an ecstatic smirk. No question about it—'Heaven on Earth.'

"Your belly a balloon," Meow said, once again foregoing her grammatical English to delight him yet another way. "I lift your crazy-colored shirt and give balloon belly big kiss."

"Later honey. You know how excited I'll get."

She gave a knowing nod.

"I want to know this," Dude said. "Why do young Thai chicks go for older men?"

Without hesitating, Meow said, "My big, big honey, Thai men like to have more than one wife. Not all Thai men, but many have girlfriend number two, girlfriend number three. And a Thai woman has to do almost everything asked of her by her husband. Not all Thai men make commands and demands, but many do. It's Thai culture, my big, big honey." All this in perfect English.

I asked the cat's Meow if I could verify her answer to Dude's question with my truth detector.

She nodded.

I took out Knowing Nose and displayed it.

George, Abe, and Dude did not know what the dangling object was. From Meow's expression, she already knew about its mysterious power.

Dude was given a demonstration—regarding his age, the American state he lived in, and whether he loved Meow—that convinced him of the crystal's accuracy.

I asked Knowing Nose if Meow's answer had been truthful.

"It's saying affirmative," Dude said, obviously awed by what was happening.

"Meow," I said, dangling Nose in its Knowing position. "Do you swear to tell the whole truth and nothing but the truth?"

She nodded and then gazed at Nose in amusement as I repeated the question.

"Meow," I said, "tell us the reasons why you and many Thai women go for older *farang* men."

She listed her reasons:

"Old man die fast," she said in bad English, making the '*boom-boom*' gesture and pointing to Dude's heart.

"Old man have money."

With that, Dude took out his wallet, fat with 50- and 100-dollar notes and wads of 1,000-baht notes. He fanned them out and indicated that she help herself.

Meow *waied* Dude and extracted three 100-dollar bills and then kissed him on both cheeks.

"Old man has no choice if he wants to get a girl," she continued. "He must pay to have romance. Nothing for free."

Dude peeled off five 100s and stuffed them in her bra. Once again, she *waied* him.

"Thai girls get more freedom with *farangs*. Thai leash short. *Farang* leash long. Thai women think have *farang* boyfriend or husband *cool*. You know what I mean?"

Once again, Knowing Nose verified that Meow had been truthful in her replies.

"You're walking around," I said to Meow, "with your trophy on parade for all your friends to see."

On the table, she pushed one of the 100s at me. I pocketed it before Dude could swipe it from me.

"The *farang* is a status symbol," I said.

She nodded as she licked the cucumber that was flavored by Pimm's Cup Number Seven. She tousled his toupee again. He loved it. She rumpled his Hawaiian shirt that clashed violently with his plaid shorts. He loved it.

Dude ordered another round of drinks. George, Abe, and I chose Pimm's Cup Number Seven with the cucumbers. Tasty.

Dude said he wanted to ask the pendulum some important questions that might affect his life.

He wanted to know if he was head over heels in love with the cat's Meow.

"But you already know that," I said.

"I know that I know. I want to have it confirmed by that cosmic wonder device you're holding."

'Yes,' emanated from Knowing Nose.

That tickled him. Next on Dude's agenda: should he marry her?

'No.'

"Why not?" he asked.

Dude was told that a yes-no question had to be put to the 'Power.'

He requested that I re-phrase the question.

"Knowing Nose," I said, "are Dude and Meow compatible?"

'No,' with vigor.

I asked if the two were sexually compatible.

'Yes.'

Does she want his money?

'Yes.'

Dude flashed his wad again. He told her to take as much as she pleased.

Meow withdrew only a modest three 100s from the seemingly inexhaustible account.

"See," Dude said, thrilled. "She could have taken the whole amount."

I asked for silence. "Knowing Nose, was Meow deceiving Dude by taking less?"

"Of course I was deceiving him," Meow volunteered.

'The Power' confirmed her remark.

"Knowing Nose, does Meow want to marry Dude?"

'No.'

"Meow," I said, "can you explain why you refuse to marry this wealthy real-estate tycoon?"

She explained that because of the way she takes care of his erotic needs, he would die soon.

Once again, her honesty thrilled him.

◆

The next day, George reported that Dude and the love of his life had checked out. They had left Pattaya unannounced. No forwarding address was given.

Six months later, I decided to check on Dude via Knowing Nose.

"Is Dude still alive?"

'Yes.'

"Is he with Meow?"

'Yes.'

"Are they living in Thailand?"

'No.'

"Are they living in the USA?"

'Yes.'

Six months from now, I will check them out again.

◆

My friend Humbert from Aussieland lives in Pattaya. When I visited him, he told me about someone that I had to include in this story. "We'll check it out, Richard. Follow me. This girl is precious. She loves her job."

Humbert took me to Pattaya's promenade, where we met nineteen-year-old Kinjiew (Loves To Eat 'You Know What). She happily admitted to being a *dokthong* ('slut').

Humbert was right.

She also admitted that she loves her job.

Kinjiew and her mother and younger sister (fourteen) hang out on the promenade in Pattaya. In this competitive business, instead of waiting for a tourist to approach her, Kinjiew latches on to male passers-by. This spider-in-waiting thrusts her body against her potential customer. Unashamedly, she giggles. Unashamedly, she maneuvers her glory to his. She nods triumphantly to her mom and sister, who will wait for her to return from the 'boudoir.' Hand-in-hand, she jaunts along, leaving a wake of laughter that is music for her mother and sister. Kinjiew is proud to be the breadwinner for her once-poor family from a small village in Isaan.

◆

With the exception of Holland and Germany, all other countries in the world outlaw prostitution. As we know, there is a difference between breaking the law and enforcing it. In New York State, it is against the law even for a father to diaper his baby. Yet, no father has had the 'cuffs' put on him. In Thailand, the legal age of consent is eighteen. Sex with minors is viewed as statutory rape.

Many foreigners, and most Thais, conveniently believe that prostitution in Thailand began during the late 1960s and early 1970s, at the height of the Vietnam War, when the US military began shipping in GIs for R 'n' R in Pattaya. It is true that the bar scene grew rapidly as a result of this, but prostitution, in its many forms and guises (more than Europeans could possibly imagine), has been alive and flourishing in the kingdom for many centuries. The Siamese didn't need white folk to introduce them to the idea of paid sex.

Pattaya was, at that time, not much more than a sleepy fishing village. Word got around that more money could be made by bargirls as the Americans kept coming.

Come to Pattaya!

After the USA was defeated by the Vietnamese, the tourism floodgates opened for Thailand. American, Australian, German, Japanese, and UK entrepreneurs began building hotels, condos, homes, entertainment palaces, go-go bars, beer bars, plus venues for the gay crowd.

In Thailand, being gay or a *katoey* (a 'ladyboy,' or transsexual) is not a cultural taboo. Gays and ladyboys are not only tolerated in Thai society, they are accepted. Many become well known in TV and entertainment circles. No gay Thai person is ashamed of his or her sexual preference. It's common for a gay man or woman to introduce a partner to family, friends, and co-workers. No need to "hang down your head, Tom Dooley."

There is controversy about the number of sex workers in Thailand. Since it's illegal, the government doesn't want to talk about the number of practicing prostitutes in the kingdom. To do so would be an admission that the authorities recognize an illegal profession. Better to take the ostrich position on this sensitive issue. The monkey position ('see no evil') works, too.

The numbers game fascinates me. According to Bernard Trink, the former columnist for the *Bangkok Post* and a legend in his own time, the figure is 1-3 million sex workers in the kingdom of 60 million. According to the authors of *Guns, Girls, Gambling, Ganga*, figures have been compiled by various NGOs and social workers. Most sex workers come from the age group 15-29. The best 'guesstimate' is that 2-2.8 million in this age category are sex workers. The three researchers quoted another source that reported 700,000 sex workers in 1991.

Veerasit and Brown, another team of researchers, applied ethnographic methods to the numbers game and came up with a figure of 150,000-200,000 in the 15-29 age range. This amounts to 6.3-8.3 percent of females in that group.

Of all the sex establishments studied, none would admit that they employed minors. The *Guns, Girls, Gambling, Ganga* authors had this to say: "Officials avoid probing about child prostitution, as they know that they will not get co-operation from either the owners of sex establishments or the local police."

The number of sex establishments throughout the kingdom in 1996 was 7,310. This figure was provided by the three Thai researchers, who reported that private membership clubs (of which there are many hundreds) were not included in the "sex establishments." Also excluded were the freelance and casual sex workers (school and college students, and housewives, seeking extra income).

◆

Another delightful paradox in Thailand is the fascination with virginity. When my good friend, Atip Muangsuwan (the Forrest Gump of Thailand) celebrated his thirty-first birthday, I asked if he was still a virgin.

181

"Richard, I am virgin until I marry my true love."

I gave him the pendulum test. He passed.

One of my Thai dance partners celebrated her thirtieth birthday. She too, was a virgin. She too, passed the test.

My first Thai-language teacher, Partee, was a 21-year-old virgin when she taught me in 2001. I had a lunch date with her in February 2006.

"Partee, you still a virgin?"

"Of course," she said, smiling.

I asked if I could tickle her.

"Cannot touch me. I'm virgin."

She too, passed the pendulum test.

On many occasions before I met Lek Lick, my current girlfriend, I went out with Thai women who brought along a chaperone—a girlfriend, sister (even mother and brother on one date.)

I asked each of my friends why so many virgins in the magical kingdom?

The Forrest Gump of Thailand, as stated above, wanted to save and savor the moment for his wedding night.

Partee told me she was also saving herself. "It's my wedding gift."

In the magical kingdom, unlike the West, virginity is sacred for women *and* men.

Sometimes a Thai cannot be touched. How sweet—a Thai treat is reserved as a precious wedding-night present.

The Saturday Expats
Club In Pattaya

"EXPATS HELPING EXPATS." Those three words from a friend made me take notice about two unusual social clubs.

In 2000, as a newcomer to the magical kingdom, I decided to check out the two "Expats Clubs" based in the seaside resort of Pattaya, my third favorite city in the magical kingdom after Bangkok and Chiang Mai.

In some respects, the Saturday morning club is similar to the Sunday morning club. Both have the same motto. Both provide important services to the community. Club volunteers teach English conversation at schools; take orphan children on outings and throw parties at the orphanage; and raise monies for charitable organizations.

The club puts out a weekly newsletter of fifty pages. The front page is in English. The back page is in German. There is an English section, a German section, a section in Danish, and a big section in the Thai language. The Saturday morning club even has its own television station that broadcasts 24 hours a day, seven days a week. The station features guest speakers, Thai and foreign, who are also interviewed for their comments on important events in the community.

Authors of novels and non-fiction books also make regular appearances. The writer with the most appearances is Christopher G. Moore. Featured speakers have included the police chief of Pattaya; the governor of Chonburi province, where Pattaya is located; the mayor; medical specialists; and other dignitaries and professionals, foreign or Thai, who have exciting jobs or are able to shed light on topics of interest to expats.

When ships of the British Royal Navy and the US Navy anchor off Pattaya, they are greeted by auxiliary members of the Pattaya Expats Club. Leading the delegation is Alex Leicester, a former officer in the Royal Navy.

"When in a foreign port," Alex said, "the Royal Navy aids the community."

The former officer provided examples. In Sri Lanka, Malaysia, Singapore, Hong Kong, and Thailand (and other ports), the British sailors provide hard labor during shore leave. They repair orphanages, fix what needs to be fixed in schools, hospitals, and other buildings. The American Navy also provides labor of love upon docking on foreign shores.

The volunteers of the Expats Club keep track of the ships that are due to arrive. "We are happy to report," Alex said, "that the British and American navies have always obliged us."

Applause and foot stomping came from the audience when Alex announced this fact at one of the Saturday meetings. "Our club helps other expats and the community," he said.

◆

I have been to the Saturday morning meetings a number of times. The average attendance is 130. To accommodate the members and friends, the ballroom and entire second floor of the Grand Sole Hotel on Pattaya's Second Road are booked.

A regular and popular speaker and entertainer extraordinaire at the Expats Club is "Sombat." In his early thirties, he has the enviable moniker of "Pop psychologist," meaning that he presents the viewpoint of Thai people and Thai culture.

Sombat's theme is that there are different standards in Western and Thai culture. "For example, you say two plus two equals four," he said, in terrific English, when I met him at one of the meetings. "Thai people say, not so. Three plus one equals four."

It's not that Thai people are contrary. Instead, the pop psychologist is demonstrating that Thai people are playful and flexible. It also means that an argument can be worked out without rancor or fists.

An American resident told the audience about an incident he had experienced with a 'baht bus' driver. Knowing the ways of Pattaya, the man, upon alighting from the pick-up truck 'bus,' paid the customary ten baht for the one-kilometer ride from Soi 5 to Soi 7. The driver was enraged. He ran after the customer and shouted in Thai.

•

"He probably cursed you," Sombat said.

The American continued. So upset was the driver that he threw the ten-baht coin at the customer. The coin fell to the ground. Rather than try to talk to this ill-tempered man, the American proceeded on his way to a store. When he came out, the coin was still on the ground.

The stunned American asked the pop psychologist for an explanation.

"First of all," Sombat said, "there is no excuse for his bad behavior. It is my wish that when a bad apple shows up, that a foreigner does not think that this kind of behavior is normal. This ill-mannered man is a very bad example of Thai people."

He added that, by throwing the coin on the ground, the driver showed disrespect for the king, whose image is on all monetary units.

"That man," Sombat went on, "insulted you, a Western guest, and he insulted our king and the country."

The pop psychologist surmised that the mean-spirited driver had had a fight with his wife the previous night. He took his feelings out on the passenger.

Another expat presented the pop psychologist with his dilemma. When a money matter arises, his Thai wife's relatives go to her. He wanted to know why the people don't approach him.

"It's better that your wife talk to the big ATM machine."

That brought howls.

Another gent in the audience was upset that his Thai wife receives many phone calls from her friends and relatives. After hanging up the phone, his wife is invariably sad for the rest of the day. She refuses to tell what's wrong.

"Sombat, do you know what's wrong?"

"Good and bad things happen to all of us every day. When bad things happen, your wife's family and friends tell her the bad things. You can tell your wife that it's better to remain silent when something goes wrong. There's no need to broadcast the woes of the day. Instead, they might consider broadcasting the *joys* of the day. Sad people create sadness. Happy people create joy for others."

Sombat continued: "Let me tell you about meanness. In Thai society, we respect our elders. Even if they are mean, we treat them with respect."

Someone at my table said, "In the USA, we don't treat our elders with respect, even if they are not mean."

Another expat pointed out that Pira Sudham, the novelist, has some of his characters refer to Westerners as "apes" and "gorillas with hair."

"Sombat," the expat said, "do Thai people continue to call us by those names?"

Sombat laughed. "That was true upcountry in the old days. Thai people had never seen *farangs*. Today, in the cities, even upcountry, white-skinned people are not unusual anymore.

When asked how he got his name, "Pop Psychologist," Sombat said that he had worked as a tour guide for many years. He loved to talk psychology and philosophy with his guests. But he quit the tour business when he decide it would be more fun to hop on a motorcycle taxi and take passengers around the city.

The Saturday morning club has devised a clever system for keeping people in their seats for the duration of the meetings, which can last two hours. Their trick? Door prizes, including made-to-measure shirts and slacks; restaurant dinners; free pizza delivery; and a host of other enticers contributed by the sponsors who loyally support the club.

The club has also come up with another method to promote its TV and newsletter operations, in addition to providing revenue for its extensive operations. The foyer outside the meeting room has tables that promote goods and services. The products range from distilled water and medicinal items to restaurants, entertainment, legal services, computer services, spa and health clubs.

At all the meetings, Thai legal people man a table. They provide a free one-hour consultation, answering questions about how to obtain a visa for a Thai girlfriend or wife, or how to buy property legally in Thailand.

That's what the Expat's Club is all about—expats helping expats; Thais helping expats; and expats helping Thais.

The Sunday Expats Club In Pattaya

ONE SUNDAY MORNING, Drew Noyes, the club's MC at the time, taught me and a group of other expats a valuable lesson about Thailand through his masterful method of storytelling.

"Many expats and visitors to the kingdom," Drew said, "have the mistaken notion that all the women of Thailand are eager to sell their body."

Drew said that some ignorant Westerners approach women in cafés, restaurants, on the street, on buses, on trains. "They say something like, 'I dig you, babe. How much for short time with you? How much for all night?'"

The women being insulted in this manner are likely to be respectable workers in offices, shops, or department stores.

"What's remarkable," Drew said, "is that Thai people exhibit tolerance in this circumstance. They attribute the insults to our ignorance."

Drew sipped a glass of water and then came the teaser: "What would happen if this occurred in my country, the USA, or in the UK, or Germany?"

Hands flew up.

"In Texas, we'd tar and feather the bastard."

The soft-spoken Drew asked, "Would you give the offender due process?"

"Do you mean would I or my friends issue a warning?"

Drew nodded.

"Fuck due process."

The audience laughed.

"In New York City," someone said, "we'd take the dude to a high-rise building and hold his feet while his body dangled in mid-air."

"Then what would you do?"

"I'm not sure. Maybe let go."

Applause from the audience.

A lady expat told us of an incident that had occurred a few days before, when she was on a cruise boat on the Mekong River. Nine drunken Brits were trying to make out with the Thai women on board. When the women refused to talk to them, the drunken tourists became nastier and meaner. The Thai men began talking among themselves. This amounted to an emergency session.

Five Thai men of slim physique stood up. One of them said, "If you men don't get off at the next village, we will toss you off."

"Oh, yeah, you and how many others?"

There was more conversing among the five Thai men. Then other Thai men came from the upper deck. Their leader said, "We changed our mind."

The Brits chugged their Heineken and chuckled.

"Instead of tossing you off at the next village," the Thai said, "we've decided to take you into the jungle."

"You and who else?" the Brit leader said, standing up. The others also stood. All towered above the Thai men. "Let's teach these five fools a lesson," came a taunt from one of the other drunks.

"Yeah," the leader said, "let's toss them into the river."

Five more Thais joined the group. Then another five. The cruise boat slowed to a crawl. Crew members brandishing crowbars and other persuasive objects, joined the party.

The audience at the club cheered when the lady expat gave the clincher: "The nine drunks sobered up. Without a word, they got off the boat at the next village."

◆

"There is no sick body, only a sick mind."

That was a quote in one of the club's weekly newsletters in 2005. Robert Morgan, a New Yorker, had worked wonders, the newsletter announced, on Wall Street; he became a millionaire by the age of 25. Satisfied with his material gains, glamorous women, and his *GQ* image, Robert Morgan (AKA "Finklepuss"—a name derived from a fictional autobiography he is working on) then decided it was time to "experience the wonders of the spirit." He had abandoned the financial world and entered the spiritual world. The New Yorker studied under masters in healing, yoga, and the meditation arts. He became an expert in reflexology. Using his corporate savvy, he set up shop in Beverly Hills, Bali, India, Nepal, Japan, and Thailand. An admirer of the 'Gentleman from Nazareth,' Finklepuss had even completed a forty-day fast.

"We make ourselves sick and we can make ourselves better," was another quote about the feature speaker from New York who would appear at the club soon. He also promised to show the expats "how to get rid of fear."

I took an early morning bus from Bangkok to Pattaya and arrived at the Henry J. Bean restaurant a few minutes before the featured speaker took the mike.

To my astonishment, the tables on the orchestra level were filled; the balcony that encircled three sides of the orchestra level was filled with expats; the booths on the other levels were also occupied. I had expected a turnout of thirty or forty; instead, there were more than 100.

Alan Sherratt, the MC, made several brief announcements and then, with zest, introduced the entrepreneur turned healer. "Robert Morgan was the youngest man to become a licensed broker on the New York Stock Exchange," Alan said.

That drew immediate attention from the expats, who ranged in age from early-forties to mid-seventies.

Alan added that Robert Morgan had studied in India for four years. He started a successful herbal and reflexology business. He practiced with healers in Bali for three years, where he ran a successful import-export firm. He prospered for five years in Japan, studying with

Japanese healers and selling healing products and organic food. He had moved to Thailand five years before, and has a private practice in Chiang Mai.

"One more pertinent fact before our speaker comes to the podium," Alan said. "His Christmas bonus during his days on Wall Street amounted to the staggering sum of 70,000 US dollars."

Applause and sighs of "wow."

But instead of standing up at the podium to deliver his talk, Finklepuss had the mike brought to him. Dressed casually in a Hawaiian shirt, his physique and mannerisms reminded me of Dustin Hoffman. He leaned back in his chair, and said, "I was a Wall Street hustler for five years and a real-estate broker in New York City, my hometown. After making my mil, I decided to put my energy into the world of the spirit."

Perhaps he sensed that the expats wanted him to talk more about his business experience and his adventures as a capitalist. He leaned back again and almost tipped over. "A powerful urge raged within my heart," Finklepuss said. "The mystery of Wall Street had been revealed. The mystery of the mind now beckoned me to ponder its secrets."

He took a sip of water and said, "The body is not sick. The mind is sick."

Gasps from the expats.

The speaker fingered the glass of water. His dramatic pause lingered on.

MC Alan got up, stroked his Van Dyke beard, and said, "Robert, excuse me for interrupting. How does the mind get sick?"

I detected a glint of glee in Finklepuss's eye. The New Yorker was a master at working the audience.

"Not only is it a good question, MC. It's a *great* question. The mind gets sick from cultural conditioning. The mind gets sick from society's belief system that is instilled into the child at an early age."

"I'll buy that," the MC said.

"The sick mind has been disconnected," Finklepuss said, "from the spirit mind that is free from sickness or disease. We have been culturally conditioned to accept the fact that the body is subjected to disease and that we are pitiful victims. It's drummed into us that we are human. I contend that we are *more than human.*"

I was waiting for an uproar of protest. Or a murmur that indicated discontent. But the expats were in rapt attention.

Finklepuss explained that all of us have fear in our lives. There's fear of getting sick, fear of losing money in investments, fear of losing our hair, fear of aging. Fear of losing our boyfriend or girlfriend.

"Now for the good news," he said. "I will show you a simple technique to get rid of fear in your life."

The New Yorker told the audience about a power technique that's been around for 5,000 years. The simple ritual takes a mere two minutes. It's done before going to sleep and upon awakening.

The audience leaned forward in anticipation.

The entrepreneur turned healer held up his right hand to the audience and displayed his five fingers. We were told that the thumb signifies the brain. The forefinger signifies the lungs. The middle finger, the small intestine; the ring finger, the kidneys. And the pinky represents our heart.

"Now," Finklepuss said, "we're ready to do one of the most important power exercises on the planet."

He displayed both hands to the audience and placed the thumb of each on the forefinger and said, "*Sat.*" He asked us to imitate him. He then pressed the thumbs of his left and right hand against the middle finger of each hand and said, "*ta.*"

The audience did likewise.

He put his thumbs against the next two fingers in turn and continued with "*na*" and "*ma.*"

The audience followed. We said "*Sat ta na ma*" twelve times loudly.

"Now we will do it in a whisper. Follow me."

To my surprise, the expat members performed the physical and vocal ritual with him. I didn't think that many Western expats would be spiritually inclined. The *sat ta na ma* mantra was repeated softly twelve times, with the pressure of the thumb against each of the other fingers in sequence with each syllable.

He told us that this was acu-pressure being applied to the corresponding body organs.

During the second and final round of the ritual, three men at a nearby table laughed in an obvious attempt at ridicule. The derisive ones were glared at, resulting in them succumbing to peer pressure and 'silence on the set.'

The ritual to eliminate fear over, Finklepuss asked if anyone had a physical problem.

A hand immediately went up. It was a woman. "Robert," she said, "I have arthritis in the fingers of both hands."

"Thanks for being courageous and speaking up. Let me read from the book I refer to as the healing bible—Louise L. Hay's, *Heal Your Body*." He held up a copy of the healing book. "I have ten copies left. See me later if you want to have it. Bargain-basement cheap."

The New Yorker turned the pages of the slim volume. Finding the appropriate place, he said, "First I'll give you the bad news, then the good news."

He read: "Arthritis. A desire to punish. Blame. Feeling victimized."

The woman was disheartened.

"Now the good news. You are to say this with confidence and conviction."

He read: "I see with love and understanding. I hold all of my experience up to the light of love."

The woman felt better.

After a few more questions, Alan, the MC, took the mike and said, "One more question and we'll go to the open forum."

A hand was raised. "Sir, what's your definition of spirituality?"

The New Yorker answered: "One who sees his or her connection with humanity, the animal kingdom, and the cosmos. All is one."

During the open forum, I went to the table where the New Yorker was talking to several people who wanted to sign up for a reflexology seminar he was giving the next day. I got there in time to buy the last copy of *Heal Your Body*.

When my turn came, I introduced myself as a fellow New Yorker. I told the speaker I was impressed by his forty-day fast and reminded him that Jesus said that those coming after him would perform greater feats than he did.

"Yes, I remember the classic comment."

"Do you plan to let yourself be killed *a la* Jesus and then rise in three days. Perhaps, unlike Jesus, you will let your re-appearance be seen by *all* the people instead of only the inner circle?"

"How rude of you to say that," an expat said.

Three others at the table agreed with him.

Finklepuss smiled and shook my hand. "You know, that very question has been on my mind for some time."

That's when Finklepuss and I became friends.

◆

He's been called "the John Steinbeck of Thailand," and his own life is like a Horatio Alger story. The rags-to-riches tale occurred in Isaan, Thailand's poor northeastern region. Pira Sudham has achieved international fame for his novels *Monsoon Country* and *The Force Of Karma*. He is also a master short story writer.

Two of Pira Sudham's short stories are embedded in my mind— "A Thai Woman In Germany" and "Two Thai Women."

The Expat Club's online newsletter announced that Pira Sudham would be the guest speaker in January, 2006. An admirer of his work, I went to the dinner honoring the distinguished candidate for the 1990 Nobel Prize for Literature. He did not win that prize, but even being considered for it is an honor of a lifetime.

Fourteen were present at the intimate dinner in Pattaya. Not only did I meet Pira Sudham, I also talked to Louis Royal, an American physician and teacher of English literature at a university in Bangkok. It was Dr. Royal who compared Pira Sudham to Steinbeck in *Thoughts*, a journal published by Chulalongkorn University in Bangkok.

Like Steinbeck, Pira Sudham is the 'Voice of Conscience' for the downtrodden and impoverished people of Thailand. Steinbeck placed the responsibility for America's unfortunates on the bankers. Pira Sudham says that Thai politicians, greedy corporate moguls, and the Thai education system are the culprits that keep the downtrodden down. According to the author, the Thai education system focuses on rote memorization; this robotic approach has made Thai people "mindless" (a word he often uses) citizens who have been trained to become submissive and obedient. Like machines, the mindless carry out the dictates of their masters. From an early age, the Thai people are taught not to be inquisitive, not to question authority, and to look upon the powers-that-be with respect and awe.

In Pira Sudham's view, all this has changed since the advent of the international schools that abound in Bangkok and other major cities in the kingdom. Some Thai citizens study abroad—in Japan, Australia, New Zealand, the US, the UK, Germany, and other Western countries—and they change from being mindless to masters of their own destiny. Impoverished but intellectual Thais can also study abroad thanks to the funding and scholarship programs of other countries.

Pira Sudham himself has established a foundation that provides students with funds to study in other countries. At the time I met him, his organization was supporting 86 Thai students abroad. He has been hailed for helping Thai university students learn to think critically and become 'mindful' instead of 'mindless.' Some professors at universities in Thailand now include Pira Sudham's haunting works in their English programs.

The author's works are written in English. While his novels and short stories have been translated into many languages, it is odd that, as late as 2006, they have not been translated into his native language. Pira Sudham told the expats that this is by design.

Like Steinbeck, Pira Sudham talks softly but carries a big pen, demonstrating yet again that the pen can be mightier than the sword.

◆

Aside from the weekly writers' group, the Sunday Expats Club also has interest groups in meditation, computers, and discussion. The meditators meet weekly for a half-hour guided meditation session followed by a social gathering. In order to promote a better understanding of Thailand, Thor Halland, an historian from the UK, has delivered lectures to the discussion group on the history of the country from its infancy to the present day. He presents his material with a comic and theatrical touch.

When a newcomer attends one of the Saturday or Sunday meetings, or any of the interest groups, he or she will marvel at the expats' exuberance.

They unashamedly toast Thailand by counting their blessings for living in a land they call paradise.

The Mystery Of
The Jumbo Queen

MAY 1ST, known in many countries as May Day or Labor Day, is also the day when Thailand's "Miss Jumbo Queen" is crowned.

According to the promoters of this recently established event, the purpose of the Miss Jumbo Queen pageant is to "find a lady of sufficient talent and proportions to lead the Jumbo Banquet and represent Thai elephants as an ambassador of elephant conservation in collaboration with the Elephant Alliance of Thailand."

According to a CNN reporter: "Only in Thailand could a contest of this kind be done."

At the 2004 contest, six members of the media were huddled at the breakfast table in the sumptuous banquet hall of Samphran Elephant Park and Zoo in Nakhon Pathom province, just west of

Bangkok. The six of us were among the early arrivals before 'The Happening.' One of the journalists whispered into my ear: "I have inside information on who the winner is."

He succeeded in drawing my attention. "This is off-the-record, you understand?" he added, taking in a mouthful of boiled rice.

"Are you joking or serious?" I asked.

"Not joking."

Was this going to be a story behind the story? I mused.

The source, who insisted on remaining anonymous, claimed that he had knowledge of the 2004 Miss Jumbo Queen winner before the official announcement would be made.

According to the organizers, as stated in the various press releases that were issued in the promo packets, the judges—ten of them— would not make the official announcement until the talent contest ended at one o'clock in the afternoon, which was four hours away. One of the judges was a producer of TV dramas for Channel 3 in Bangkok. Another judge was a director of the Tourism Authority of Thailand.

My source, in a conspiratorial tone, told me the number of the winning contestant for this year's event. He also disclosed the reason why the judges voted for her. She was "statuesque," had a winning personallity, and a sense of humor.

"What about the other winners?" I asked. (There were prizes for various categories in the pageant.) "Do you have inside information about them, as well?"

The anonymous source claimed that he had no knowledge about the other winners.

If true, the news would create a scandal and tarnish the annual event, now in its tenth year. It was a tropical and torrid sunny day, but the negative news succeeded in pouring rain on the parade.

A gentle breeze nudged us as we made our way through the grounds of the Samphran Elephant Park. People began to fill the seats in front of the massive stage that contained a catwalk. The staff escorted the six of us, along with new arrivals of the press corps, into the dressing room of the chubby ladies.

There they were, the twenty finalists who survived the cut from 120-plus contestants, sitting in front of mirrors, as make-up artists touched up faces and curling irons created waves of hair cascading down to the shoulders of some of the bulging beauties.

I talked to Miss Supinda Rithichan, aged 29, 107 kilograms, and 1.69 meters tall. She received a Master's degree in business education from Srinakharinwirot University in Bangkok, and was an instructor in marketing at the Thai Business Administration College. I learned that she had designed and cut the material of her costume, which consisted of several hundred zippers in bright orange. She was a cross between a pumpkin and a poppy field in bloom. She was a Van Gogh painting in three-dimensional form, radiating sunlight in all directions. The dazzling costumes inspired me to make a mental note to the promoters that they consider including a category of 'Best Costume' for next year's event. But if my anonymous source's rumor turned out to be true, that the contest was rigged, there might not be one next year.

Miss Supinda giggled when flashlights popped and TV cameras closed in on her, along with reporters, microphones in hand. She smiled as she applied the final touch to her costume—a blonde wig. Color upon color, adding more sunshine to an already blazing woman.

Through my interpreter, Wapawee Techawangtsam, nicknamed Tik—thank Thai culture for using nicknames—I learned that Miss Supinda, number 14 of the elite circle of twenty, believed that "large ladies have beautiful hair, faces, and skin because of high nutrition." I studied her face. Smooth, clear, sexy with unmistakable beauty. She maintained that diets succeeded only in blemishing the skin and making it dry. "I eat many times," Supinda said. "It makes me more beautiful and more powerful."

Number 14 was asked what her reaction would be if she was not among the seven winners. "Not a problem. I made many fat friends here. I have had many good experiences, too."

Spoken like a true winner.

Her dream was to market a product for chubby ladies and start a service to help them become fashion models.

Other contestants were in the final stages of being touched up, powered, brushed, sprayed, pinned together, and massaged on the upper back. If they were nervous, it didn't show. Perhaps the paparazzi had a mesmerizing, magical effect on them. I focused on their faces—all were smooth and free of blemishes; many of them were beautiful.

◆

The event was about to get underway. I watched the drama unfold from the vantage point of the press section that surrounded the stage on three sides. Each of the twenty finalists appeared separately on stage. The protocol required them to stride down the catwalk, introduce themselves briefly, and answer difficult questions from the two MCs that were submitted by the panel of ten judges. The finale was a talent contest where each lady gave a two-minute performance.

I decided to tell Tik (who worked for Syllable, the PR firm that promoted the Miss Jumbo Queen pageant), and solicit her reaction about the rumor that the winner had already been decided.

"Who told you that?" Tik asked.

"A source that wishes to remain anonymous," I said.

Instead of Tik being ticked off, she gave me a Mona Lisa smile that said many things, including 'my dear boy, you think you know something.'

Still 'Mona Lisa-ing' me, she said, "Can you tell me the name of the winner?"

I gave her the name and number.

After pondering the information, Tik said, "When Miss Jumbo Queen is announced, I will tell you why your source thinks the rumored one should be the new Queen."

Back to the action on stage:

"How did you get to be so chubby?" asked one of the MCs. The question (submitted by the judges) was directed to Miss Bangon Waiyawong, aged 34, 170 kilograms, on a frame of 1.70 meters. She replied in a calm manner: "Twelve years ago, I weighed 52 kilos."

A gasp from the audience.

I didn't understand the reason for the gasp. Nor did I understand the laughter that followed her subsequent remarks.

I asked Tik to explain the audience's reaction.

"Her boyfriend likes chubby ladies," Tik said. "He encourages her to eat all the time."

Hmmmm, I mused. Bigger is better.

"When she reached 100 kilos, she asked her boyfriend if she should stop. 'Eat more,' he told her."

My burning question was: "Are Miss Bangon and her boyfriend still together?"

"Yes," Tik said. She added that the contestant looked like a goldfish in her costume. How true.

The heaviest jumbo of them all made a suggestion to the judges. "Perhaps next year you will have a contest for the 'Jumbo King' of Thailand."

Much applause and cheering from the press and audience.

Miss Bangon then performed *Sao Pichit Rumphun*, a sexy dance.

Another contestant, Miss Aroonwan Savatanan, commented that her boyfriend pleaded with her to *lose* weight. She said her goal was to reduce herself from 95 kilos to seventy. Aged thirty, Miss Aroonwan majored in music and received a bachelor's degree in education. She worked as a teacher at Wat Bang Pla School in Nakhon Pathom province, the home of the Samphran Elephant Park and Zoo.

The MC presented her with a tough question: "As a teacher, what would you do with kids who make problems?"

"I would try to discover the reason or reasons for what troubles the student," Miss Aroonwan replied. "Then I would point out her good qualities and help her focus on her strong points."

Truly cool under fire.

She performed on traditional Thai musical instruments like the *khru* and *ranaat*.

One of the MCs presented a major obstacle to Miss Artpapat Boonnarung, aged 22, 95 kilograms, 1.70 meters. She received a degree in business administration from Sripathum University. Her father owned a special-effects production company. She worked as an aerobics instructor, make-up artist, and dancer. The no-win question posed to Miss Artpapat: "If you had three wishes, what would they be?"

"That there be peace in southern Thailand, good health for my parents, and that the Miss Jumbo pageant be known all over the world."

Her performance was lip-synching and dancing to "Let's Get Loud" by Jennifer Lopez.

A thunderous ovation greeted the appearance of Kanittha Namkong, aged 27, 112 kilograms, just over the 1.60-meter mark. She stood on the stage dressed as a little angel—making her the biggest little angel ever seen in the celestial or earthly realm. She gave a comic performance as she lip-synched to "Stupid Cupid."

The contestants displayed their talent, imagination, creativity, stagecraft (including camera-friendliness), and thrilled the audience with performances like the Spanish dance *pasa doble*, in which one contestant portrayed the matador and her partner appeared to play the bull. There was a gymnast twirling a ten-meter ribbon with artistry and charm; and another chubby girl lip-synched to a Madonna hit.

Then the time came when the MCs would announce 'And the winner is. . . .'

The trumpets blared as the moment arrived. The coveted prize of "Miss Jumbo Queen" would be declared last, after the other prizes had been announced and awarded.

The "Supermodel" winner—the heaviest of the jumbos—was Bangon Waiyawong. She had tipped the scales at 170 kilograms. No contest.

Voted for by the media, the "Miss Photogenic" prize went to Yotaka Jullobon.

The "Miss Popular Winner" was Nutthida Wongsomboon. This prize was determined by phone-in voting.

The overall second runner-up was Piyacha Chawooti.

First runner-up went to Surassamee Holaputra.

And the winner of the 2004 Miss Jumbo Queen was Artpapat Boonnarong, number 13.

Excited by the announcement, I poked Tik in the belly. "My anonymous source," I said, "was wrong."

She explained that the misinformation given to me by the media man might have been based on his *hope* that Rudhukhon Oranseattakul would take the top prize. Rudhukhon, nicknamed Yui (Chubby), was the darling of the public and the sentimental favorite. A nursing student at the prestigious Mahidol University Medical School, she had had to overcome opposition by the Nursing faculty. At the time of student admission a year before, she had been considered grossly overweight at 97 kilograms. Refusing to take no for an answer, she proposed that she be admitted on the condition that she would lose ten kilos during the academic year. By giving up chocolate ("Quite difficult, you know") and saying no to other sweets as well as limiting her food intake, she shed twelve kilograms in one year, exceeding the ten-kilo target that was set as the goal for continuing in her studies.

"I love nursing," she told the audience during the interview-talent phase of the contest. "By being a heavyweight, I can lift fat patients. Three nurses are not required. I'm strong."

What was her reaction to coming up empty in this year's beauty pageant? She failed to win in any of the categories. Her response: "I am proud to be a participant and to show that heavy people can break barriers. Before me, there were no fat nurses."

A true role model for all chubbies and a source of admiration for others.

In closing, hail to Artpapat Boonnarong, the 2004 Miss Jumbo Queen—aged 22, 95 kilograms, 1.70 meters tall.

The reigning Queen's first job was to escort her entourage to the elephant ground, where 25 pachyderms, including a five-month-old baby, would feast on their favorite fruits and vegetables. During the year, the 'Queen,' as ambassador for the Elephant Alliance of Thailand, would promote the cause of the animals.

"Elephants work very hard," said Pichai Chaimongkoktrakul, chairman of the Jumbo Queen contest. "And they make people happy. Did you know, they can even swim underwater for prolonged periods."

How do they do it? By using their trunks as a snorkel.

The new Miss Jumbo Queen was crowned and given a fat check of 50,000 baht. (In 1997, the first Jumbo Queen's prize money was just 2,500 baht). She was adorned with a colorful sash, and presented with a jumbo-sized trophy, a skin-care voucher valued at 30,000 baht from a luxury spa, a three-day holiday in Chiang Rai with a round-trip air ticket, and a sack bursting with cosmetics. Fifty thousand baht is a lot of spending power in the Land of Smiles—a mini-fortune.

After the crowning of the new Queen, I prowled through the press section, on the lookout for my anonymous source. Nowhere to be found.

Thailand's Magnificent Musical Monarch

KING RAMA IX, when he acceded the throne in 1946, promised the people of Thailand that he would rule on their behalf. His reign would be characterized by improving the conditions of the poor.

The first true test of his promise came in October 1973, when unprecedented democracy demonstrations were held in Bangkok, demanding an end to the military rule of the reviled Field Marshal Thanom Kittikachorn. The hated military leader came to power through a coup. He responded to the peaceful demonstrators with force. Seventy people were killed in cold blood—something not seen in Thailand for many years.

Despite the slaughter, more people poured into the streets. Further bloodshed was averted by His Majesty's behind-the-scene machinations, including his withdrawal of support for the oppressive military regime and an appeal to the public via radio and television. These actions by King Rama IX were his first foray into a political crisis. On October 14th, 1973, General Thanom resigned and left the country. Gentle persuasion worked.

The events of October 1973 were a revolution in Thai politics. For the first time, the urban middle class, led by students, had defeated the combined forces of the old ruling class and the army, and had gained the blessing of the king for a transition to full democracy. This was symbolized by a new constitution which provided for an elected parliament.

That's one reason why this Westerner is fond of His Majesty—the longest reigning monarch in the world. He lived up to his inaugural promise that he was for the people.

The second test came in February 1991, when generals Sunthorn Kongsompong and Suchinda Kraprayoon staged another coup d'etat. The military brought in a civilian prime minister, Anand Panyarachun, who was still responsible to the military in the form of a "National Peacekeeping Council" with General Sunthorn as its chairman.

Anand's anti-corruption measures proved popular, but in March 1992, the strongman General Suchinda stepped in and took power himself, breaking a promise he had made to the king.

General Suchinda's coup brought hundreds of thousands of people out onto the streets in the largest demonstrations ever seen in Bangkok. The second people's uprising was led by the former governor of Bangkok, Chamlong Srimuang.

Suchinda brought military units personally loyal to him into the city and tried to suppress the demonstrations by force. Suchinda's action resulted in a bloody massacre in the heart of the city, in which hundreds died. Several hundred demonstrators disappeared. To this day, none of the missing have been found. Thousands were hospitalized.

The Royal Thai Navy mutinied in protest, and the country seemed on the verge of civil war. The king intervened. In a televised broadcast, he reprimanded both Suchinda—who promptly resigned—and the protest leader, Chamlong. The prestige of Rama IX was further heightened, and the king was elevated even further in the eyes of the public. He enjoys semi-divine status among the Thai people.

His Majesty's second intervention proved that once again, he lived up to his 1946 promise that he was for the people.

◆

Trouble has been brewing in southern Thailand for many years. The Muslim population of the south does not trust the Thai establishment. Violence erupted in four southern provinces bordering Malaysia in 2004. King Rama IX called for more sensitivity to the needs of all Thai citizens of the southern provinces. Perhaps in the near future, the problems plaguing the region will be resolved. If and when that happens, I am convinced the public will appreciate the efforts of His Majesty, and Her Majesty the Queen, in trying to reconcile the differences and bring harmony and goodwill to the region.

◆

The year was 1996. It was the golden jubilee of King Rama IX. His fiftieth year on the throne. The following tribute to His Majesty was delivered on the floor of the United States Senate by Senator Max Baucus of Montana.

Mr. President of the United States,

Today, King Bhumibol Adulyadej of Thailand begins the fiftieth year of his reign. It is my great pleasure to join Montana's Thai community in offering him congratulations and best wishes.

King Bhumibol took the name Rama IX and opened the Ninth Reign of the Chakri Dynasty on June 9th, 1946, just a few months after the end of the Second World War. At the time, like the rest of Southeast Asia, Thailand faced severe questions. They arose from the end of colonialism in neighboring countries; the rise of radical ideologies worldwide; and endemic poverty, illiteracy, and illness.

Today, Thailand is one of the anchors of the modern, prosperous Southeast Asia. Bangkok has become one of the world's great cities and commercial centers. The Thai political system is evolving into a stable parliamentary democracy; in fact, a new political campaign opens today as candidates across Thailand file their papers to run for Parliament. And the Thai economy grows by seven percent or more every year.

Much of this extraordinary success is due to the wise guidance of King Bhumibol. The king has led by example. He has embodied the ten traditional moral principles of Buddhist kings: charity toward the poor; morality; sacrifice of personal interest; honesty; courtesy; self-restraint; tranquility of temperament; non-violence; patience; and impartiality in settling disputes.

And he has led by action. Together, King Bhumibol and Queen Sirikit have devoted decades to improving the lives of Thai people in rural and impoverished regions. They constantly travel the country's 76 provinces, meeting with villagers and staying close to the people. The results are obvious in improved public health, the spread of education to all Thai children, and the renewal of traditional crafts and textiles.

Mr. President, King Bhumibol is now the longest-reigning king of Thailand. And history is certain to rank his reign with those not only of the greatest Thai monarchs of the past—Ramkamhaeng, creator of the Thai alphabet; Naresuan and Phra Narai in the Ayuthaya era; Mongkut and Chulalongkorn in the last century—but the great constitutional monarchs of the world and the democratic leaders of modern times.

It is my great pleasure to join all the Thai Montanans in congratulating King Bhumibol as he begins the fiftieth year of his reign, and looking forward to many more to come.

Thus ended the tribute made in 1996. In 2006, in the sixtieth year of His Majesty's reign—his fifth twelve-year cycle, which is very significant in Asian astrology—more deserved accolades were bestowed on the great monarch. Members of almost every royal family in the world came to Thailand in June 2006 to pay their respects and enjoy a rare and spectacular 'royal barge ceremony' on the Chao Phraya River.

During the three-day public holiday to commemorate his coronation, almost every single Thai person on the street could be seen wearing a yellow T-shirt, shirt, or blouse with a royal emblem on the breast—yellow being the color traditionally associated with Monday, the day of the week on which he was born. It was a wonderful and stunning display of love and reverence toward the great king.

BBC TV in Thailand paid an endearing tribute to His Majesty. In a weeklong salute during the June anniversary, video clips of Rama IX were shown regularly. The screen titles said: "His Majesty, the King of Hearts."

◆

To Mo Tejani, my friend, a jazz historian, and a long-time resident of the Land of Smiles, I asked, "Why do you like King Rama IX?"

"As you know," Mo said, "I'm a jazz lover. The king not only loves jazz, he is a master of three instruments—saxophone, piano, and guitar. That in itself is an extraordinary feat."

Mo continued: "He also composes music. I don't know how many love songs he's written, but it must number more than fifty."

"Those are good reasons," I said.

"Did you know that the king of Thailand has jammed with the royalty of jazz?"

I told Mo I wasn't aware of that.

Mo said that the king has jammed with Dizzy Gillespie, Benny Goodman, Count Basie, Miles Davis, Louis Armstrong, and Dave Brubeck. Some of the jazz greats came to Thailand to 'Hail the King' by giving special performances.

Another friend told me that he liked and respected the king because he was an excellent photographer and, like Winston Churchill, is an artist with the brush. "And he composed a full symphony," he added. "I don't know the name, but it was performed with a full orchestra."

At the Bangkok Film Festival in 2006, I asked filmmakers for their thoughts on the world's longest-reigning monarch. "There is the king of Denmark, the king of Spain, the king of Sweden, the king of Saudi Arabia, the Queen of the UK, and various others," said Antonio Pineda, the author of *The Magick Papers*. "But there is only one *cool* king, and that's the king of Thailand."

The king of Thailand is a legend in his own time. He serves with dignity and humility, and he has proven time and again that he is a king for all the people of the kingdom.

What is curious about the king 'upsetting the apple cart' of dictators is that, when he came to the throne in 1946, Thailand's monarchy was in a state of decline. The new king was very young and was viewed as a puppet whose strings could be pulled by the military. To their horror, the two tyrannical regimes had to dance to the tune played by the 'Magnificent Musical Monarch.'

Glossary

boom-boom—Thai euphemism for sexual intercourse.

chai yo—cheers.

farang—a Caucasian foreigner.

Isaan—the northeastern region of Thailand
(culturally more Lao than Thai).

jai dii—literally 'good heart.'

katoey—a transsexual (ladyboy).

khlui—traditional bamboo pipe.

Lanna—the ancient kingdom and culture of northern
Thailand, centered around Chiang Mai.

Loy Kratong—November full moon festival in which
candles, coins, flowers, and incense are

placed in a banana-leaf float and set adrift

(along with the sponsor's woes and wishes)

upon a river, lake, or other watercourse.

ramwong—a traditional folk dance of

northeastern Thailand and Laos.

ranaat—traditional type of xylophone.

sanuk—fun.

soi—a lane or smaller road leading off a main thoroughfare.

Songkran—April water festival celebrating

the traditional Thai New Year.

wai—traditional greeting, or expression of respect or

gratitude, in which the palms are pressed together,

prayer-like, in front of the chest, nose, or forehead

(depending upon the status of the recipient).

Directory

The Saturday Expats Club in Pattaya
(Now meets on Sunday)
www.pattayaexpatsclub.com

The Sunday Expats Club in Pattaya
(Continues to meet on Sunday)
www.pattayacityexpatsclub.com

The Spiritual Banker, Tony U-Thasoonthorn
www.intlmedclub.org
infoUSA@intlmedclub.org
01 622 4507

THAI TOUCH

Robert Morgan (AKA Finklepuss)
Reflexologist and Herbalist
(Lives in Chiang Mai and gives seminars
and private sessions in Bangkok.)
01 992 3714

La Rueda Latin Dance Club
Sukhumvit Road, Soi 18
www.salsabangkok@hotmail.com

Fogo Vivo Brazilian restaurant and La Rueda Latin Dance Club
(For Argentine tango lessons)
The Inter-Continental Hotel, Chidlom
www.tangobkk@hotmail.com

About The Author
(Abbreviated)

My father was a numbers runner for the mob in New York. He did something bad and was told, "Git outta town. Udderwise."

Titles from Paiboon Publishing

Title: **Thai for Beginners**
Author: Benjawan Poomsan Becker ©1995
Description: Designed for either self-study or classroom use. Teaches all four language skills- speaking, listening (when used in conjunction with the cassette tapes), reading and writing. Offers clear, easy, step-by-step instruction building on what has been previously learned. Used by many Thai temples and institutes in America and Thailand. Cassettes & CD available. Paperback. 270 pages. 6" x 8.5"

Book   US$12.95   Stock # 1001B
Two CDs US$20.00   Stock # 1001CD

Title: **Thai for Travelers** (Pocket Book Version)
Author: Benjawan Poomsan Becker ©2006
Description: The best Thai phrase book you can find. It contains thousands of useful words and phrases for travelers in many situations. The phrases are practical and up-to-date and can be used instantly. The CD that accompanies the book will help you improve your pronunciation and expedite your Thai language learning. You will be able to speak Thai in no time! Full version on mobile phones and PocketPC also available at www.vervata.com.
Book & CD   US$15.00   Stock # 1022BCD

Title: **Thai for Intermediate Learners**
Author: Benjawan Poomsan Becker ©1998
Description: The continuation of Thai for Beginners . Users are expected to be able to read basic Thai language. There is transliteration when new words are introduced. Teaches reading, writing and speaking at a higher level. Keeps students interested with cultural facts about Thailand. Helps expand your Thai vocabulary in a systematic way. Paperback. 220 pages. 6" x 8.5"

Book   US$12.95 Stock # 1002B
Two CDs   US$15.00 Stock # 1002CD

Title: **Thai for Advanced Readers**
Author: Benjawan Poomsan Becker ©2000
Description: A book that helps students practice reading Thai at an advanced level. It contains reading exercises, short essays, newspaper articles, cultural and historical facts about Thailand and miscellaneous information about the Thai language. Students need to be able to read basic Thai. Paperback. 210 pages. 6" x 8.5"

Book   US$12.95 Stock # 1003B
Two CDs   US$15.00 Stock # 1003CD

Title: **Thai-English, English-Thai Dictionary for Non-Thai Speakers**
Author: Benjawan Poomsan Becker ©2002
Description: Designed to help English speakers communicate in Thai. It is equally useful for those who can read the Thai alphabet and those who can't. Most Thai-English dictionaries either use Thai script exclusively for the Thai entries (making them difficult for westerners to use) or use only phonetic transliteration (making it impossible to look up a word in Thai script). This dictionary solves these problems. You will find most of the vocabulary you are likely to need in everyday life, including basic, cultural, political and scientific terms. Paperback. 658 pages. 4.1" x 5.6"
Book   US$15.00 Stock # 1008B

Title: **Improving Your Thai Pronunciation**
Author: Benjawan Poomsan Becker ©2003
Description: Designed to help foreingers maximize their potential in pronouncing Thai words and enhance their Thai listening and speaking skills. Students will find that they have more confidence in speaking the language and can make themselves understood better. The book and the CDs are made to be used in combination. The course is straight forward, easy to follow and compact. Paperback. 48 pages. 5" x 7.5" + One-hour CD
Book & CD   US$15.00 Stock # 1011BCD

Title: **Thai for Lovers**
Author: Nit & Jack Ajee ©1999
Description: An ideal book for lovers. A short cut to romantic communication in Thailand. There are useful sentences with their Thai translations throughout the book. You won't find any Thai language book more fun and user-friendly. Rated R!
Paperback. 190 pages. 6" x 8.5"
Book   US$13.95 Stock #: 1004B
Two CDs   US$17.00 Stock #: 1004CD

Title: **Thai for Gay Tourists**
Author: Saksit Pakdeesiam ©2001
Description: The ultimate language guide for gay and bisexual men visiting Thailand. Lots of gay oriented language, culture, commentaries and other information. Instant sentences for convenient use by gay visitors. Fun and sexy. The best way to communicate with your Thai gay friends and partners! Rated R!
Paperback. 220 pages. 6" x 8.5"
Book   US$13.95 Stock # 1007B
Two Tape Set   US$17.00 Stock # 1007T

Title: **Thailand Fever**
Authors: Chris Pirazzi and Vitida Vasant ©2005
Description: A road map for Thai-Western relationships. The must-have relationship guidebook which lets each of you finally express complex issues of both cultures. Thailand Fever is an astonishing, one-of-a-kind, bilingual expose of the cultural secrets that are the key to a smooth Thai-Western relationship. Paperback. 258 pages. 6" x 8.5"
Book   US$15.95 Stock # 1017B

Title: **Thai-English, English-Thai Software Dictionary**
       for Palm OS PDAs With Search-by-Sound
Authors: Benjawan Poomsan Becker and Chris Pirazzi ©2003
Description: This software dictionary provides instant access to 21,000 English, Phonetic and Thai Palm OS PDA with large, clear fonts and everyday vocabulary. If you're not familiar with the Thai alphabet, you can also look up Thai words by their sounds. Perfect for the casual traveller or the dedicated Thai learner. Must have a Palm OS PDA and access to the Internet in order to use this product.
Book & CD-ROM US$39.95 Stock # 1013BCD-ROM

Title: **Thai for Beginners Software**
Authors: Benjawan Poomsan Becker and Dominique Mayrand ©2004
Description: Best Thai language software available in the market! Designed especially for non-romanized written Thai to help you to rapidly improve your listening and reading skills! Over 3,000 recordings of both male and female voices. The content is similar to the book Thai for Beginners, but with interactive exercises and much more instantly useful words and phrases. Multiple easy-to-read font styles and sizes. Super-crisp enhanced text with romanized transliteration which can be turned on or off for all items.
Book & CD-ROM US$40.00 Stock # 1016BCD-ROM

Title: **Lao-English, English-Lao Dictionary for Non-Lao Speakers**
Authors: Benjawan Poomsan Becker & Khamphan Mingbuapha ©2003
Description: Designed to help English speakers communicate in Lao. This practical dictionary is useful both in Laos and in Northeast Thailand. Students can use it without having to learn the Lao alphabet. However, there is a comprehensive introduction to the Lao writing system and pronunciation. The transliteration system is the same as that used in Paiboon Publishing's other books. It contains most of the vocabulary used in everyday life, including basic, cultural, political and scientific terms. Paperback. 780 pages. 4.1" x 5.6"
Book   US$15.00 Stock # 1010B

Title: **Lao for Beginners**
Authors: Buasawan Simmala and Benjawan Poomsan Becker ©2003
Description: Designed for either self-study or classroom use. Teaches all four language skills- speaking, listening (when used in conjunction with the audio), reading and writing. Offers clear, easy, step-by-step instruction building on what has been previously learned. Paperback. 292 pages. 6" x 8.5"
Book   US$12.95 Stock # 1012B
Three CDs   US$20.00 Stock # 1012CD

Title: **Cambodian for Beginners**
Authors: Richard K. Gilbert and Sovandy Hang ©2004
Description: Designed for either self-study or classroom use. Teaches all four language skills- speaking, listening (when used in conjunction with the CDs), reading and writing. Offers clear, easy, step-by-step instruction building on what has been previously learned. Paperback. 290 pages. 6" x 8.5"
Book   US$12.95 Stock # 1015B
Three CDs   US$20.00 Stock # 1015CD

Title: **Burmese for Beginners**
Author: Gene Mesher ©2006
Description: Designed for either self-study or classroom use. Teaches all four language skills- speaking, listening (when used in conjunction with the CDs), reading and writing. Offers clear, easy, step-by-step instruction building on what has been previously learned. Paperback. 320 pages. 6" x 8.5"
Book   US$12.95 Stock # 1019B
Three CDs   US$20.00 Stock # 1019CD

Title: **Vietnamese for Beginners**
Authors: Jake Catlett and Huong Nguyen ©2006
Description: Designed for either self-study or classroom use. Teaches all four language skills- speaking, listening (when used in conjunction with the CDs), reading and writing. Offers clear, easy, step-by-step instruction building on what has been previously learned. Paperback. 292 pages. 6" x 8.5"
Book   US$12.95 Stock # 1020B
Three CDs   US$20.00 Stock # 1020CD

Title: **Tai Go No Kiso**
Author: Benjawan Poomsan Becker ©2002
Description: Thai for Japanese speakers. Japanese version of Thai for Beginners. Paperback. 262 pages. 6" x 8.5"
Book   US$12.95 Stock # 1009B
Three Tape Set US$20.00 Stock # 1009T

Title: **Thai fuer Anfaenger**
Author: Benjawan Poomsan Becker ©2000
Description: Thai for German speakers. German version of Thai for Beginners. Paperback. 245 pages. 6" x 8.5"
Book   US$13.95   Stock # 1005B
Two CDs US$20.00   Stock # 1005CD

Title: **Practical Thai Conversation DVD Volume 1**
Author: Benjawan Poomsan Becker ©2005
Description: This new media for learning Thai comes with a booklet and a DVD. You will enjoy watching and listening to this program and learn the Thai language in a way you have never done before. Use it on your TV, desktop or laptop. The course is straight forward, easy to follow and compact. A must-have for all Thai learners! DVD and Paperback, 65 pages 4.8" x 7.1"
Book & DVD   US$15.00   Stock # 1018BDVD

Title: **Practical Thai Conversation DVD Volume 2**
Author: Benjawan Poomsan Becker ©2006
Description: Designed for intermediate Thai learners! This new media for learning Thai comes with a booklet and a DVD. You will enjoy watching and listening to this program and learn the Thai language in a way you have never done before. Use it on your TV, desktop or laptop. The course is straight forward, easy to follow and compact. DVD and Paperback, 60 pages 4.8" x 7.1"
Book & DVD   US$15.00   Stock # 1021BDVD

Title: **A Chameleon's Tale - True Stories of a Global Refugee -**
Author: Mohezin Tejani ©2006
Description: A heart touching real life story of Mo Tejani, a global refugee who spends thirty four years searching five continents for a country he could call home. Enjoy the ride through numerous countries in Asia, Africa, North and South America. His adventurous stories are unique – distinctly different from other travelers' tales. Recommended item from Paiboon Publishing for avid readers worldwide. Paperback. 257 pages. 5" x 7.5"
Book   US$19.95   Stock #1024B

Title: **Thai Touch**
Author: Richard Rubacher ©2006
Description: The good and the bad of the Land of Smiles are told with a comic touch. The book focuses on the spiritual and mystical side of the magical kingdom as well as its dark side. The good and the bad are told with a comic touch. The Sex Baron, the Naughty & Nice Massage Parlors, the "Bangkok haircut" and Bar Girls & the Pendulum are contrasted with tales of the Thai Forrest Gump, the Spiritual Banker of Thailand and the 72-year old woman whose breasts spout miracle milk. Paperback. 220 pages. 5" x 7.5"
Book   US$19.95   Stock #1024B

Title: **How to Buy Land and Build a House in Thailand**
Author: Philip Bryce ©2006
Description: This book contains essential information for anyone contemplating buying or leasing land and building a house in Thailand. Subjects covered: land ownership options, land titles, taxes, permits, lawyers, architects and builders. Also includes English/Thai building words and phrases and common Thai building techniques. Learn how to build your dream house in Thailand that is well made, structurally sound and nicely finished. Paperback. 6" x 8.5"

Book   US$19.95   Stock #1025B

Title: **Retiring in Thailand**
Authors: Philip Bryce and Sunisa Wongdee Terlecky ©2006
Description: A very useful guide for those who are interested in retiring in Thailand. It contains critical information for retirees, such as how to get a retirement visa, banking, health care, renting and buying property, everyday life issues and other important retirement factors. It also lists Thailand's top retirement locations. It's a must for anyone considering living the good life in the Land of Smiles. 6" x 8.5"
Book   US$19.95   Stock #1026B

Coming Soon in 2007

Title: **Lao for Travelers** by Saikham Jamison
Title: **Vietnamese for Travelers** by Jake Catlett
Title: **Cambodian for Travelers** by Richard Gilbert
Title: **Burmese for Travelers** by Gene Mesher
Title: **Paragon English Vol. 1** A textbook for Thai people to learn English

Title: **Living Thai**
           -Your Guide to Contemporary Thai Expressions- Vol. 1
Author: Benjawan Poomsan Becker ©2007
Description: This series of books and CDs is a collection of numerous words and expressions used by modern Thai speakers. It will help you to understand colloquial Thai and to express yourself naturally. You will not find these phases in any textbooks. It's a language course that all Thai learners have been waiting for. Impress your Thai friends with the real spoken Thai. Lots of fun. Good for students of all levels.

Title: **Thai Law for Foreigners**

Author: Ruengsak Thongkaew ©2007

Description: Thai law made easy for foreigners. This unique book includes information regarding immigration, family, property, civil and criminal law used in Thailand. Very useful for both visitors and those who live in Thailand. Written by an experienced Thai trial lawyer. It contains both the Thai text and full English translation.

Title: **The Smart Medical Tourist**

Authors: Julie Munro and Hari DePietro ©2007

Description: A unique guide book for travelers looking for medical treatment that is affordable, safe, stress-free, with the most advanced medical technology and world class medical providers. This well researched book from medical tourism insiders includes the history, development and economics of medical tourism, stories of medical travelers for both cosmetic surgery and specialized surgery including heart and orthopedic procedures, how to choose a doctor, planning ahead, comparing costs, getting medical and travel insurance, and much more. Covers Thailand, Singapore, Malaysia, India, Dubai, South Africa, Brazil, Mexico, Costa Rica, and other countries.

Title: **How to Establish a Successful Business in Thailand**

Author: Philip Wylie ©2007

Description: This is the perfect book for anyone thinking of starting or buying a business in Thailand. This book will save readers lots of headaches, time and money. This guide is full of information on how to run a business in Thailand including practical tips by successful foreign business people from different trades, such as guest house, bar trade, e-commerce, export and restaurant. This is an essential guide for all foreigners thinking of doing business - or improving their business - in Thailand.